thelibrary
don't be lost for words

Glennyce Eckersley is an international angel expert and the author of many successful books, including An Angel at My Shoulder and Saved by the Angels. She lives in Manchester, UK.

Gary Quinn is a spiritual teacher, leading intuitive life coach and popular author whose books include May the Angels Be with You and Living in the Spiritual Zone. He is the founder of Our Living Centre in Los Angeles, California.

Glennyce and Gary are the co-authors of An Angel Forever and Angel Awakenings. They have appeared many times in the media individually and together, and run successful workshops on both sides of the Atlantic.

Believe and Receive

Bring the Guidance and Wisdom of the Angels into Your Life

Glennyce S. Eckersley
and Gary Quinn

RIDER

LONDON · SYDNEY · AUCKLAND · JOHANNESBURG

3 5 7 9 10 8 6 4

Published in 2007 by Rider, an imprint of Ebury Publishing
A Random House Group Company

Copyright © Glennyce S. Eckersley and Gary Quinn, 2007

Glennyce S. Eckersley and Gary Quinn have asserted their right to be
identified as the authors of this Work in accordance with the
Copyright, Designs and Patents Act 1988

The Random House Group Limited Reg. No. 954009

Addresses for companies within the Random House Group can be
found at
www.randomhouse.co.uk

A CIP catalogue record for this book is available from the
British Library

The Random House Group Limited supports The Forest Stewardship
Council (FSC), the leading international forest certification organisation.
All our titles that are printed on Greenpeace approved FSC certified paper
carry the FSC logo. Our paper procurement policy can be found at:
www.rbooks.co.uk/environment.

Printed and bound in Great Britain by Cox & Wyman Ltd, Reading,
Berkshire

ISBN 978-1-8460-4086-3

To buy books by your favourite authors and register for offers visit
www.rbooks.co.uk

*To the stars and angels in
all our lives*

Contents

Introduction

Seven Stars

The morning star of this new day,

looks on a different world.

Little Book of Miracles

This book will take you on a celestial journey around seven special stars. As you will discover, each star represents particular angelic powers and embodies key qualities such as self-belief, love and peace. Through intriguing stories, inspiring quotations and a variety of practical exercises, you will find out how to tap into these celestial powers and bring them into your own life.

Why seven stars? First, let us turn to the number seven. As authors and angel experts, we have become increasingly aware of and fascinated by the number seven. And in this we are not alone: more and more people appear to be studying the qualities of this intriguing digit, as shown by the increasing number of magazine articles and workshops offering insights into it. Seven is of course a hugely significant number in literature, music (there are seven basic notes) and mathematics, and it is often thought of as being a particularly holy number, sacred in many senses of the word, seven surfaces being regarded as significant in all major religions and in many ancient beliefs.

Many people think that seven is a number that has mystical properties. Whether we realise it or not, it dominates many aspects of our existence. According to Shakespeare's *As*

You Like It, even our lives can be measured in seven ages: the infant, the schoolchild, the lover, the soldier, the justice, the pantaloon and the second childhood. In ancient wisdom, the soul of man was believed to consist of seven properties, which were under the influence of the seven planets or 'stars'. Similarly, there were the ancient seven pillars of wisdom. In yogic teaching, seven basic colours are attributed to the chakras (the energy points in the body), and there are those who are able to see the seven colours as they manifest in personal auras. There are of course seven colours in the rainbow.

According to the Bible, the average life span of a man was three score years and ten, making the number 70 or seven decades. The Creation story in the Bible features the seven days in which the firmament was completed, and it is said that God created seven levels of heaven, hence the expression 'in seventh heaven'. In the Old Testament, the Pharaoh of ancient Egypt had a dream featuring seven years of plenty, followed by seven years of famine. The leader Moses, who led the Israelites out of Egypt and received the Ten Commandments, was of the seventh generation after Abraham. In the Judaic tradition, the Jewish festival of Sukkot was to last seven days by God's command, with Yom Kippur and Rosh Hashanah occurring in the seventh month of the Hebrew calendar. When a close relative dies, many Jewish families will still sit *shiva* for seven days. Moving to the New Testament, the final book of the Bible, Revelation, describes a scroll with seven seals, which inspired film director Ingmar Bergman's film *The Seventh Seal*. Even today, each week in the Western calendar has seven days, with the seventh day being 'holy' in Christian tradition.

The eighteenth-century mystic and theologian Emanuel Swedenborg wrote extensively about the significance of the number seven. In *Arcana Celestia* (vol 1) he talks about the seven days of creation and the seven stages of regeneration of the human spirit. He writes about the significance of numbers in the Bible, including the number seven: 'When seven occurs, instead of seven, what is holy comes to the angels.' Swedenborg taught that there are groups of angels in heaven that are constantly aware of people, especially children, reading the Bible. When the word seven is read it implies holiness to the angels. This is why the seventh day, for instance, is regarded as holy.

The Rev. David Gaffney, a Swedenborgian scholar and musician, teaches these revelations in his workshops and notes that: 'The seven notes of the musical scale also represent both the seven stages of creation of the cosmos and the seven stages of creation of the human spirit.' There are in fact seven archangels: Michael, Jophiel, Chamuuel, Gabriel, Raphael, Uriel and Zadkiel. (As we will see in Star of Trust, each angel is associated with a particular colour.) Seven notes are also fundamental to the ancient but recently rediscovered nine-pointed enneagram, which is becoming so popular with all kinds of groups as a tool for character analysis.

So the number seven continues to intrigue us to this day with its many associations. However, an equally interesting influence lies in the heavens, with the stars. From early childhood, many of us discover a fascination with the stars that never fades. Indeed, who can look up at a night sky filled with glittering constellations without feeling awe and wonder? As human beings, we are quite literally bursts of starlight – sharing our atoms with the material of the stars, as we do indeed with all living things. (The atoms we share are simply arranged in a different order.) The connection is very real and the saying 'look to the stars' highly appropriate when we want to boost our connection with nature and increase our self-belief.

Indigenous peoples set great store by the heavenly constellations, as did ancient mariners. Particularly revered, especially by the Native Americans, was Ursa Major, or the Great Bear, which is composed of seven stars. It was believed that the stars were actually people who had died. In Henry

Wadsworth Longfellow's famous poem *Hiawatha* the young Hiawatha is told that at midnight, after her death, his grandmother has been thrown into the sky and that the beautiful star he can see is his grandmother.

The wonder of the stars is also reflected in the science of astrology. Many of us check our horoscope diligently, even though we may not believe it, and consider the practice just a little bit of fun. However, the study of the planets and their influence on our lives goes much deeper than might be suggested by most horoscopes in magazines and newspapers. Astrologers claim that their detailed astrological charts show how the planets influence not only each individual but also world events.

In our consideration of the number seven and the stars, we cannot forget the angels who have links with both the mystical digit and the heavens. When working on this book, it seemed a logical step for us to combine the special number seven with angels and stars. As you will see, these angelic stars and their properties are connected to demanding areas of modern life that sometimes require a touch of extra inspiration. So many people are looking for a little guidance and support, which we fervently hope will be found within these pages. (And we should just like to point out that the first edition of this book is published in 2007 ... the number seven again!)

In each chapter, the practical exercises are designed to encourage you to engage creatively with your situation, to give you more insight, courage and harmony in your life, including the freedom to let go of things that aren't working for you, to ask for what you deserve to experience, and to be the kind of person you know you should be. (Please don't be afraid of failing, or of doing any of the exercises wrong – that's impossible!) The meditations in each chapter will enable you to tune into your inner thoughts and intuition, as well as into the angelic powers already present in your life – but which you may not always be aware of. If repeated or posted prominently where they catch your eye, the affirmations will help to strengthen your links with the celestial realms, while the Angel Top Tips and Divine Stars offer heavenly food for thought. The true stories show the angels at work in the lives of ordinary people around the world.

We would like to add that – as the title suggests – the whole concept of this book is based on the principle of believe and receive. Today many people refer to this principle as 'Cosmic Ordering', which might seem like just another modern fad to perhaps be ignored. Cosmic Ordering is, however, merely a new title for an ancient belief system. In his gospel, St Matthew quotes Jesus as saying, 'Ask and it shall be given unto you.' Where exactly does He say this? Why, in chapter seven, verse seven, of course!

In *Believe and Receive*, seven chapters will help you navigate your way around seven angelic stars in a magical journey that could enrich your life for ever . . .

Happy star-gazing!

Glennyce S. Eckersley and Gary Quinn

❧ 1 ☙

The Star of Self-Belief

*If you have made mistakes, there is always
another chance for you . . . you may have a
fresh start any moment you choose, for this
thing we call 'failure' is not the falling
down, but the staying down.*

Mary Pickford,
American actress, 1893–1979

Self-belief is one of the building blocks of a happy life. To enjoy a full, positive existence and to create positive change in the world around us, we must first have self-belief. If we believe in ourselves and believe the angels are there to help us, the sky is literally the limit as to what we can achieve. However, in order to experience true self-belief, we may have to do a little work first in order to change ourselves from within.

You may already be familiar with the expression 'you are what you eat'. Let's take that one step further by saying 'you are what you think'. The mind is a very powerful tool, as everything we do or say to implement change in our lives originates from a single thought. Therefore it is important to identify what it is in life we wish to change or accomplish, for as we think it, so we will become it. To make our thoughts lead to positive changes, we have to ground them in powerful self-belief.

However, our past experiences may mean that we initially lack conviction that we can achieve our goals, and we may need to overcome the negative thought patterns that are holding us back. In such cases, this maxim can be very handy: 'Fake it till you make it'! If we give out positive vibes, not only will we be sending out the right messages to others, but we may convince ourselves in the process! Nevertheless, as we will see later in this chapter, we may have to abolish some patterns of negative thinking that condition how we respond to the world. For many of us, when things begin to look a little difficult, those all too familiar feelings of self-doubt and failure creep in. It is at this point that we need to push those negative thoughts from our minds and grasp the concept that, provided we believe in ourselves, our aims are truly possible, and then we will receive the help necessary to achieve them.

What are your own goals in life? Are they related to your career or does your personal life need serious attention? Once you have clear goals in mind, you can get to work on achieving them. The process may require patience and a little perseverance, as you will see in this chapter – after all, if you have doubted yourself for many years, it may take a little time to recover your self-belief. To get yourself motivated, pause for a moment and consider the following question: when the film of your life is played at the end of this journey, do you want it to be a boring, safe documentary? Instead, why not let it be an epic, exciting and full of evidence of gifts well used, and a record of your true appreciation of the world around you, of nature and of people?

In the matter of achieving your goals in life, it's not so much the case that 'seeing is believing' as 'believing is seeing'. With a little self-belief, what wonderful things might you see in your life? If you truly believed in yourself, what do you think you could achieve? Anything is possible . . .

By exploring the Star of Self-Belief you will discover ways to transform how you feel about yourself. You will learn how your conditioning affects your life and also discover how to prioritise your goals and then achieve them, whilst learning how to identify your true passions in life and then attract new opportunities to yourself. So don't be afraid to reach out to the future – it's only change!

✎ Angel Top Tip ✐

To strengthen your own connection with the heavens, go outside and look at the sky on a clear and starry night. Then, choose a star or even a constellation, and make it your own.
Know that whenever you gaze upon this heavenly body and ask the angels to be with you, a positive reply will be forthcoming. In turn, this practice will help to lift your spirits whenever you need a boost.

EXERCISE:
Listen to Your Body

As our lives reflect what we feel about ourselves, we must first learn to love ourselves before we can love others. This means getting to know and accept ourselves. It also means learning to listen to ourselves. Let's begin on a physical level. Quite simply – what is your body telling you?

Read through the whole exercise first and, when you have memorised what to do, begin.

Start by sitting comfortably in a darkened room. Relax into your chair, visualising a blue light at the top of your head. Picture this blue light travelling the length of your body, from the crown of your head to the tips of your toes, a short section at a time.

* Pause at your head. Do you suffer from headaches, strained eyesight? What might be causing this, do you think? How do you feel about facing the world? Accept any answers that come to you. Allow yourself to relax and visualise any tension dissolving in the blue light before moving on.

* Pause at your shoulders and the top of your back. Do your shoulders feel loose or tense? Is one side more knotted than the other? Do you feel any tension at the base of your neck? Why might this be so? What could your shoulder and upper back be telling you about the burdens that you are shouldering? Allow yourself to relax further and visualise any tension dissolving in the blue light before moving on.

* Pause at your back and midriff. Do you experience back pain or any discomfort here? What could your back be telling you about the support you need? Allow yourself to relax and visualise any tension dissolving in the blue light before moving on.

* Pause at your lower abdomen and hips. How loose do your hips feel? How comfortable do you think your position is in the world? What problems might you be trying to digest? Allow yourself to relax once more and visualise any tension dissolving in the blue light before moving on.

* Pause at your legs and feet. How tired or vital do your limbs feel? What could they be telling you about your standing and your direction in the world? Allow yourself to relax further and visualise any tension dissolving in the blue light before moving on.

✳ With time, quiet reflection on your physical being, combined with the peace that meditation can bring (see below), may help you to understand your body's messages for you, and banish your aches and pains. By becoming familiar with the ways in which your body physically embodies your world view, you will begin to identify the thought patterns that have shaped the way you live. These thought patterns form the conditioning that governs many of the ways in which you respond to the world. Once you are aware of the role that conditioning plays in your life, you will be able to take conscious steps to overcome it where necessary.

Conditioning

Self-belief is a quality that develops with us as we go through life. From our earliest childhood our self-belief may have been influenced by a variety of factors, some of which we may be aware of, such as the day-to-day routines of our homes and the demands of our upbringing, and others that may lurk below the surface of our consciousness.

Our minds are full of subconscious thoughts and attitudes, which lead us throughout the day. Do we think twice, for instance, about the direction we take on leaving home each day? Similarly, if we are experienced drivers we don't consciously think about where the clutch or the brake is in the car. We simply respond automatically. How many of us talk on the telephone whilst cooking or loading the washing machine or opening the day's mail? We do not think about each task, we are pre-programmed by our brains to get on with it. The same is true of our state of mind; we may have been programmed to think negatively in our present lives because of events that occurred many years ago in childhood.

Many of us will have been raised in environments that

didn't encourage us to think for ourselves but that urged us instead to look outwards for answers. We may have become overly dependent on others for their opinions, and thereby lost confidence in the value of our own decisions, gradually eroding our innate self-belief. We may have become fixed in the way that we view the world and how we expect life to unfold. And once we believe something, we may be tempted to shut the door to everything outside of, or opposed to, that belief and to stop enquiring about ourselves. This process is called 'conditioning' and it creates the patterns whereby we subconsciously restrict our lives. However, there are various techniques and exercises that we can use to undo some of the conditioning that ties us down. One way is simply to spring clean our minds.

EXERCISE:
Spring Clean Your Mind

This exercise is designed to help you achieve a new level of mental fitness by helping you to disentangle yourself from conditioning and from old negative habits so that you can rise into a fresh awareness. It is a process, paralleling nature, of revealing yourself to yourself. Your rewards will be new insights, improved wellbeing and increased understanding of how your life works.

You are going to explore how you currently regard self-belief by writing down detailed answers to the following questions. Please be honest without censoring yourself by being self-conscious or self-judgemental. If you don't know the answer to something, you may either have a guess at it or write 'don't know'. You may discover that spending a few minutes contemplating your thoughts before you write down the answers might have a profound effect on your life. Enjoy the questions and think without any limits, coming up with at least three potential responses for each open-ended question. What you believe is what you believe, and know that the truth you discover is your truth.

1. What problems and judgements do I have with and about my body?

2. What problems are there in my relationships?

3. What problems do I have with my finances?

4. For each problem, what would the ideal solution be?

5. What problems have I encountered in my career?

6. What is my vision of what I would like the world to look like?

7. Secretly I would love to . . .

8. If I was younger I would . . .

9. When I have more money I will . . .

10. If anything were possible, I would . . .

11. My heart's desire is for me to be . . .

12. My heart's desire is for me to achieve . . .

13. My heart's desire is for me to have . . .

14. My most important desire to fulfil in this lifetime is . . .

To acquire the awareness of the Divine, one need
not journey to any special region or place. It is
enough if the eye is turned inwards. In the
Bhagavad Gita, the inner reality, the Atma, is
described as 'splendorous like a billion suns'. But
man has not become aware of the light and
power within.

Sri Sathya Sai Baba
Religious leader and philosopher

Conditioning and the Inner Angel

Happily, we are never completely at the mercy of our conditioning, for within each one of us lies a Higher Power that
contains all the answers we need. Emanuel Swedenborg called
this power our 'Inner Angel', and claimed that the more we
'exercise' our Inner Angel the more response we will receive
from the Inner Angel in others. He taught that we are all in
fact 'trainee angels' and that we are here on earth specifically
because of the intention of the Divine to raise us to the realms
of angels in the afterlife. We are therefore all connected to the
Divine and to all of creation. Our journey in life is not only a
geographical one, but should also be an inner one, searching
for our very own inner angel.

Swedenborg also stated that we have the ability to access
this part of ourselves at any moment in order to discover
exactly what choices need to be made in our lives. Although
in these modern times the majority of us have become
distracted by the demands of daily life and unable to
recognise the true guidance of our inner angels, with a little
practice we can all open up those channels of communication
again.

Initially, this process may involve exercises that promote

self-understanding and self-enquiry, but once we start the process, the guidance of our inner angel will come to us in many forms. It can be likened to a sort of spiritual intuition, a deep feeling or inner 'voice'. As we get to know ourselves and feel increasingly comfortable searching within our own hearts and minds for the answers we need, we may even find our self-belief returning ...

To begin to connect with your own Inner Angel or intuition, find a little time to practise the exercises in this chapter. You could make a start by simply repeating the affirmation below a couple of times today.

AFFIRMATION

Today, I am blessed with the gift of confidence and all my actions have direction and purpose.

Divine Star

Changing your life can be as simple as changing your mind. If you choose to believe in life and choose to be enriched by life, you will be free to act in the fullness of any moment.

How Lynn Became a Star

So many of us go through life suffering from low self-esteem and the belief that we are somehow unworthy. When Gary and I met Lynn, we were reminded of the stories of Hans Christian Andersen. Apparently, Hans Christian Andersen was a very unattractive man physically and many of his tales were intended to encourage readers to look beyond the outward appearances of things. His well-loved story 'The Ugly Duckling' is a prime example of this philosophy. Like the Ugly Duckling in the story, Lynn was convinced she was unattractive. In fact, she was so ashamed of her appearance that she didn't even dare to apply for jobs that, with her qualifications in design, she knew she could easily perform. It is difficult to know just how or where Lynn's insecurity first took root, as she was in fact a pretty girl.

Having attended one of our angel workshops, she arrived home at the end of the day determined to ask for angelic help. Focusing on the affirmation 'My mind is at perfect ease' and lighting a candle, she meditated on the concept that freedom of thought and deed were indeed within her grasp – if she trusted her angels, she decided, her personal freedom would surely follow.

The following day, Lynn received a phone call. To her surprise, it was from a woman she had met at the angel workshop. During the lunch break, the two of them had shared their enthusiasm for the world of interior design. Impressed by Lynn's design qualifications, the woman was calling now to ask if Lynn would be interested in attending an interview for a position with her own design company. Little had Lynn realised that her lunchtime chat would lead to this outcome.

Sometime later Lynn found herself working for her new friend, happy and secure, with good prospects for promotion and a wonderful outlet for her talents. Now that her self-belief had been totally restored, her happiness allowed her beauty to shine through and she was truly transformed into a swan!

'Angels are firmly part of my everyday thinking now, and I never go to bed without thanking God for his angelic messengers, who stepped into my life when I needed them most,' Lynn confides. As she discovered, we all have inner depths as yet unplumbed; we all have greater potential than we may realise and often we are the only ones who prevent ourselves from achieving our goals.

Light tomorrow with today!

Elizabeth Barrett Browning
Poet (1806–61)

❧ *Angel Top Tip* ❧

The Universe will always support us when we commit ourselves with complete certainty, confidence and limitless trust. Then we will find the resources we need within ourselves to move into a greater sphere of action.

Tuning into the Universe

Beliefs create a cause-and-effect link between your self and the Universe. Whenever a situation doesn't work out the way you would like it to, and you are wracked by self-doubt or feel unable to move forward, you may be tempted to give up. This is precisely when you most need to realise that the angels are always with you, offering you the compassionate guidance and support you need. You are always supported by the angels and will accomplish the purpose of your life in ways you cannot even begin to imagine. If you live with this knowledge, you will find it much easier to feel positive about your situation, however difficult it appears, and to expect good things to happen in your life. The Universe will seem like a much friendlier place.

Meditation is one way to tune into the angelic realms and, believe it or not, anyone can meditate. As you will discover in the meditations in this book, you will simply need to find a window of calm and a little willpower to help you focus.

Meditation is a time of quiet, when the mind is freed from its attachment to the ravings of a world gone mad. It is a silence in which the spirit of God can enter us and work his divine alchemy upon us.

Marianne Williamson
Spiritual activist, author and lecturer

MEDITATION:
Angel of Self-Belief

Beliefs are the thought forms through which we create, interpret and interact with reality. Use this meditation to tune into the support of the Universe and commit to the belief that the angels are already there waiting to help you, thereby transcending all the expectations you've ever had. In this moment let the angelic realm transform your life.

Shut the door, turn off the phone, put the pets in another room and make sure that you cannot be disturbed for the next 20 minutes.

* Light a gold-coloured candle (if you have one) or a simple night-light. Make sure that the candle is in a safe place, that you won't be leaving it unattended and that it won't set fire to anything near it!

* Sit yourself comfortably opposite the candle, where you can focus your gaze on its flickering flame.

* Relax your hands in your lap.

* Half closing your eyes, visualise a cloud of golden energy surrounding your body, like the flame surrounds the wick of the candle.

* Open your mind and heart, and welcome in the Angel of Self-Belief.

* Repeat silently through your meditation:

  Today, I am surrounded by the love of the Universe and supported by my angels. I make the conscious choice to go forward in faith rather than backwards in fear.

* Picture each breath bringing more energy and vitality into your life. Let the golden angelic energy flow around and through your entire being.

* When you are ready, thank your angels and let yourself surface to outer consciousness.

AFFIRMATION

Today, I use the insights of timeless wisdom to light my way as I explore my real self.

EXERCISE:
Create a Self-Belief Symbol

There are other tools in addition to meditation that you can draw upon whenever you need to call on your inner resources. This exercise in particular is designed to help you tap into the feelings of being strong and in charge whenever your confidence is flagging.

You will need:

A pen and paper

A carefully chosen small object such as a pebble, a piece of yellow crystal (e.g. citrine) or a beautiful sea shell.

* Make a list of ten separate occasions when you have felt proud of yourself. If you are feeling unhappy at the moment, it might be hard at first to think of ten occasions. Persevere and allow your memory to roam as far back in time as you like. Your final list might include anything from yesterday's successful presentation, to that delicious meal you prepared, to coming second in the egg-and-spoon race when you were little. It doesn't matter if your achievement was praised by anyone else: the important thing is that it made you feel good about yourself.

* Take a few deep, steadying breaths. Pick up your object and roll it between your fingers and over your palms. Continue to hold your chosen object while you slowly read through your list for the next ten minutes. Allow yourself to revisit all those feelings and sensations you had on those occasions when you felt proud of yourself. If a negative thought surfaces, simply let it drift by and refocus your attention on the positive emotions. When you have gone over your list at least four or five times, put down the object. It is now your very own self-belief symbol.

* Place the symbol in your pocket or purse, so that whenever you next feel in need of reassurance it is readily to hand. Whenever you touch it, remind yourself of all those occasions when you achieved something to be proud of. Be confident that you can bring your own positive energy to everything you choose to undertake. With your symbol in your grasp, ask your angel to lead you to new experiences and challenges in the certain knowledge that you will be helped and encouraged every step of the way.

* And don't despair if you lose your chosen symbol – you won't lose your connection to the angels. Simply choose another object and repeat the exercise above.

Life begets life, energy creates energy. It is only by spending oneself that one becomes rich.

Sarah Bernhardt
French stage actress (1844–1923)

Stars, Angels and Goosebumps!

The angels gave Janice a special symbol of their presence when she most needed to receive one.

The move was always going to be an upheaval for Janice but the fragile state of her mother's health had placed even more pressure on her. For some time, Janice had been worried about the elderly lady, who lived thousands of miles away in the northern state of Michigan with Janice's younger sister. This arrangement had been a blessing, but now her sister had a young family and it was becoming increasingly difficult for her to cope with her mother's worsening condition. As Janice was based in the southern states of America she only saw her mother infrequently, so she had decided to move closer to her and share the caring duties. Although it meant selling her house and leaving her friends and a community that she felt very much a part of, Janice knew she wanted to help at this very difficult phase in her mother's life.

The move had taken place and one evening Janice found herself sitting in the garden of her sister's house, looking up at the night sky and wondering if she really had the inner strength for the task ahead. The two sisters remarked on how beautiful the night sky was that evening, with its brilliant stars and a huge, round moon. Suddenly, both women gasped, for there in the middle of the stars a cloud formation had appeared in the shape of two huge angels. One angel had the moon shining through as its face, whilst the adjoining cloud angel had a halo of light and two massive wings. So clear and perfect were these cloud angels amongst the moon and stars that the sisters say it gave them 'goosebumps'. A warm intense feeling of self-belief swept through Janice and she suddenly knew for certain she would be able to face the future with the angels watching over her.

I think that wherever your journey takes you,

There are new gods waiting there

With divine patience – and laughter.

Susan M. Watkins
Author

Divine Star

Each day, repeat an affirmation before you
leave the house. Be determined that the day
will contain angels and sunshine, even if
it is raining!

AFFIRMATION

*Today, I claim power to choose my
life's path in a new direction and
celebrate my life.*

*I centre my mind upon only the
positives of life.*

How Do You See Yourself Today?

We looked earlier at the thorny problem of conditioning and how it can limit our lives. The same applies to the way we judge ourselves in relation to others. There will always be people who seem to be more attractive or smarter than us; people who drive bigger cars or live in bigger houses. There will be people who have attended more prestigious schools; who have high-powered jobs and who appear to make more money in a year than we could hope to earn in a lifetime. To our eyes, these individuals may have attractive partners, brilliant children and exciting friends. Perhaps they travel to exciting, exotic places and their taste always seems impeccable. However, they too will have secret heartaches, worries and, believe it or not, from time to time they too may experience self-doubt.

So it's time to stop judging yourself in relation to others. After all, everything is relative, so begin to count your own blessings, of which you may be pleasantly surprised to find there are many. As we have already seen, you possess a powerful tool: your mind. It's time to harness that power, to know that you can change your life for ever. A positive mental attitude will ensure your success, so consider what is really important in your life and concentrate upon that. To begin with, identify one specific goal, concentrate on it, and the rest will follow.

If your body language is negative and you project the vibes of being one of life's losers, chances are that that is how others will see you too. People will read your body language, attitude and demeanour long before they talk to you. They may have already made up their mind about you before you even get a chance to speak.

On the other hand, confident body language will give a favourable impression immediately. So stand up straight and look yourself in the eye in the mirror each morning. Tell yourself you have a brand new day waiting, a blank canvas on which to write your own personal story. You are going to make the day and your story in it positive and happy. Give yourself a big smile and go out to face the world secure in the knowledge that your angel will go with you.

Lo the lilies of the field,

How their leaves instruction yield!

Hark to Nature's lesson given

By the blessed birds of heaven!

Every bush and tufted tree

Warbles sweet philosophy —

Mortal, flee from doubt and sorrow,

God provideth for the morrow.

Reginald Heber
Bishop and hymn writer (1783–1826)

You are beautiful no matter what your mind tells you.

That is a fact.

If you are aware of your own beauty

and accept your own beauty,

the opinion of others does not affect you at all.

Don Miguel Ruiz
Toltec shaman and author

❧ Angel Top Tip ☙

Flick through some magazines and
newspapers, and open your mind and heart to
the belief that life can be full of wonderful
positive things. Which photographs capture
your attention? Are there any that illustrate
your own hopes, wishes and ambitions? Cut
out a couple and place them where you can
see them each morning to remind you of how
positive and powerful you can be.

Yes, You Are Perfect!

Our ideas and thoughts often create our realities, because we
give such power to them. Have you been hanging on to
doubts and fears about the future? Those negative feelings are
all made up in your mind. You are perfect just the way you
are.

You too are unique, beautiful and talented. Beauty and
truth belong to every one of us: believe it, for truth is where
we start. Although conventional beauty may not be over-
whelmingly evident and conventional wisdom may not be
abundant in our lives, we all have our own beauty and
wisdom that are to be revered. No labels will identify you for
you are unique.

You have an invisible essence and awareness, which you
may need to tune into a little more closely. Take a moment to
listen to your heart and soul. What do you wish to gain
today? What do you want to create? What do you believe in?
If you begin to pay close attention to the spirit within yourself

and make an effort to keep the higher vibrations in your life, you shall start to see the results. Dare to be great – you have the energy and the help to achieve greatness, you only have to ask. The Universe has everything you need and your angels will make sure that you receive it if you welcome them into your life. Most importantly, banish the thought you are not worthy – you too deserve gifts from the Universal force.

Wisdom has no cleverness in it.

It is pure and simple,

and when it is practised

the results are obvious.

The Tao of Motherhood

Divine Star

Do you feel as though you are living your life in a pressure cooker? Often so many expectations are placed upon us that life appears to be an endless round of catching up. When we fail to catch up, thoughts of failure invade our minds, our self-belief drains away and we may not know where to turn. Help, however, is closer than you may think. Believe in your angel and you are off to a flying start!

What would happen if this were not done at
all? If the answer is 'Nothing would happen'
then obviously the conclusion is to stop doing it.
It is amazing how many things busy people are
doing that would not be missed!

Peter Drucker
Management consultant and author (1909–2005)

Cherish the Good Things

Shift your focus away from what is wrong or what upsets you. Instead, consciously begin to pay more attention to the good things in life. For instance, if someone pays you a compliment, rather than dismiss it out of hand, receive it gracefully with thanks, in the knowledge that it was given to you in a spirit of honest appreciation.

Your mind and body are inextricably linked. If you take care of yourself physically, you will feel good. And if you feel good physically, then it will follow that you will begin to feel more positive mentally. Pay attention to your physical wellbeing rather than your aches and pains. Start by making small changes, perhaps by eating more healthily, increasing your exercise, and finding time for proper rest and relaxation. Even if you only begin by swapping the daily chocolate bar for an apple, and by walking a little each day, the accompanying rise in endorphin levels with their 'feelgood factor' will soon kick in. Your physical health and emotional health are intertwined and when you look after your body, you will begin to feel renewed and refreshed in every area of your life.

Visualise yourself as you wish to be and how you wish other people to perceive you. Now hold that image in your mind and know that it is obtainable. If you find yourself surrounded by people who moan and groan all the time, initiate friendships with people who have a positive outlook on life and who treat you with respect.

You are special and deserving of the happiness self-belief brings. Make today the most significant of your life and prepare for change!

AFFIRMATION

Today, I use the insights of timeless wisdom to light my way as I explore my real self.

❧ *Angel Top Tip* ❧

The opportunity to experience something new is created in your mind, so use your mind to release the past and embrace something new and incredible right now. Realise that there is a Universal Law of Good that governs life. Become clear about how your thoughts and behaviour take shape in the world around you.

Prepare for Change

The past is gone; we only have today. We may have to make a concerted effort to be less negative about our lives and to overcome our conditioning, but with effort and determination we can all break away from our in-built emotions and feelings. We are all in charge of our destinies.

So often the temptation is to go through life blaming our environment, our family and even our ancestors, but that works only for so long. In the end it is up to each one of us to change what makes us unhappy in our lives.

Start today in the certain knowledge that life can be fulfilling and rewarding. Open your mind and heart to the belief that life can and will be full of wonderful positive things for you and for those you love.

Prioritise, identify one specific goal, concentrate on that and the rest will follow. Let your mantra be: *as I think, so I will become*. Truly, if you believe you can do it, you will do it! By being positive in one key area, you will give out encouraging vibes to those around you and the positive effect will spread into all other areas of your life.

All that we are is a result
of what we have thought.

Buddha

EXERCISE:
Create an Angel Journal

Many people find that keeping a daily diary really helps them to make sense of their lives. Writing down your thoughts and feelings on a daily basis will tell you a great deal about yourself, which may lead to a greater understanding of why you behave in certain ways or harbour the thought patterns you do.

You will need:

A special notebook and a good pen

A few minutes each week

In your journal, write down five sentences in response to the following statements and suggestions:

I wish to change in my life . . .

I want to achieve in my life . . .

I know that I am strong enough to . . .

I will banish negative thought at all times . . .

I will count my blessings . . .

I will appreciate myself . . .

I will ask my angels for help if required . . .

Use your journal to record daily events and unusual occurrences that might indicate the presence of angels in your life. Also use it to record your answers to the exercises in this book.

The First Steps Down the Path to Power . . .

'Believe' and 'receive' walk hand in hand; they originate from the same spark of light instilled in us at the moment of our creation. We start our life's journey loving only those in our immediate presence, but hopefully, we will end our journey loving a large portion of the entire world! Similarly, we may start our journey believing in a small way and may end our journey continually receiving from a higher power. If we have the courage to follow them to their ultimate destination, our paths in life will lead us to a higher knowledge, deeper trust and greater love, until we reach a point in wisdom where everything simply flows.

Take charge of your life; don't hide behind a job or another person. See everything as a lesson to be learned. Discover exactly what it is that you want from life, as we all need clarity before we can make any decision. Consider the choices you face, be positive about your options, then choose and believe in the knowledge that you are guided. Don't allow self-doubt to creep in, but practise trusting instead. The more you trust your inner feelings and intuition, the more you will see the results in your life.

Eventually you will become aware of the distinction between inner guidance and your own judgement system. Thoughts are in fact energy and energy is magnetic, so the more positive the thought, the more positive the energy it attracts! Happy thoughts attract happy people – it's as simple as that. Decide today what it is you really want in life. If you believe that you can have it and believe that you deserve it, you have already taken the first step towards receiving it.

AFFIRMATION

*Today, I claim power to choose my
life's path in a new direction and
celebrate my life. I centre my mind
upon only the positives of life.*

Norma's Journey

Norma is a shining example of a person who refused to be overcome by life's difficulties, and whose worldview meant that she was one of the most positive, cheerful people that I (Glennyce) have ever met, attracting a warm response wherever she went.

When Norma attended the first of two workshops I was facilitating in 2006, she declared that she would definitely come to the second workshop later that year in September. True to her word, she arrived with a large grin on her face, delighted to be there and very excited about the day. There was an aura of love and light surrounding her, even though physically she was obviously struggling. Standing and walking were proving difficult for her but the smile never left her face. She spoke positively about life and how wonderful it was, how she felt that the angels were always nearby, helping her with her journey.

However, Norma's journey was a good deal more difficult than most people attending that day would ever have suspected, because she was suffering from terminal cancer. Nevertheless, 'I see this journey as an adventure,' she said. 'I know the angels are with me on this journey and that makes me happy and positive.'

During the workshop that day, many people gravitated towards Norma. She was frequently to be found comforting those with physical problems or those who were newly bereaved. All were impressed by her inner calm, and her conviction that everything would be well. As the day came to a close and people left, everyone gave Norma a hug, silently returning some of the love she had dispensed that day.

I didn't see Norma again after the second workshop in 2006, although we chatted on the phone from time to time. Whenever I spoke to her the same calm, confident spirit always came through. I promised her I would write her story in this book as an example of self-belief even in adversity.

Indeed, I had just finished writing the opening paragraphs of her story and decided to take a break for lunch when the telephone rang. It was Norma's son, Christopher. 'My mum asked me to ring you,' he said. 'She is very close to the end and not expected to live for more than a few hours.' Even at this point, Norma wanted me to know that she was facing the end with courage, faith and dignity.

I always believe that coincidences are engineered by angels and I was very moved by the fact that Christopher's call had come just as I was writing down his mother's story. It was less than 24 hours later that Norma passed in her sleep to the next world. She was such an inspiring lady she will, I know, be greatly missed, but I hope her family and friends take comfort in the thought that she is now with the angels, where she longed to be. For me, she will always represent the epitome of self-belief with her unshakeable faith that the angels were guiding her through the most difficult time in her life.

> *Your passage through time and space is not at random. You cannot but be in the right place at the right time. Such is the strength of God, such are his gifts.*

A Course in Miracles

Belief and Self-Belief

In our experience and in that of the many people who write to us with their own amazing true stories, angels are a loving force sent by God (or a Higher Power) for our help, guidance and protection. And it seems that merely believing in them may bring benefits! Recent research has revealed that people with a religious or spiritual belief system are not only happier on the whole than the general population, but on average live seven years longer. (There is that magic number seven again.) The evidence suggests that an intact belief system leads to a move positive outlook and therefore to a healthier life. Those who are completely alone and isolated owing to their circumstances, and yet who hold on to a belief system, are motivated to recover from setbacks and illness in the knowledge that spiritually they are far from alone.

We all have to face difficulties and struggles of one type or another at various points in our lives, and it is at these points that knowing our angel is there watching over us and guiding us may steer us through.

When life presents more challenges than you can handle, delegate to God. He not only has the answer, He is the answer.

Tavis Smiley
Talkshow host, journalist and author

MEDITATION:
Shining Like a Star

This meditation is designed to help you get a sense of your own innate power and wisdom.

Sit comfortably in a place where you will not be disturbed. Relax and close your eyes.

As you close your eyes, take a long . . . deep . . . breath . . .

* Feel your body relaxing as you continue to breathe slowly and deeply. Breathing in and breathing out, release any tension and allow passing thoughts to drift away.

* In this space of peace and stillness, affirm now that you have all the answers inside you: I have all the answers I need within myself.

* Send your thoughts around your body, scanning it for tension. If there is a place in your body that you sense is undermining your self-belief, focus your attention directly on that part of your body. Take a deep breath and affirm: I have all the answers I need within myself. Now feel any doubt being released from the space within your body . . . Take a deep breath . . . allow yourself to simply let go of the doubt.

* Notice all the different points in your body now sparkling with light. Those are the sources of wisdom. Notice how more and more places within you are beginning to light up. There are millions of light sources within you. Fill your entire being with sparkling light . . .

* Feel the gratitude moving throughout your body . . . the freedom of release. Embrace the love and support you are feeling. Take a long, deep breath now, and affirm your belief in the Universe.

* As you move out of this meditation, know that you have

chosen to walk the path of belief, and that the Universe is reflecting the vision you believe.

> *For him who has*
> *no concentration,*
> *there is no tranquillity.*

Bhagavad Gita

Pam's Mysterious Feather

Pam's story shows how the angels support us even when we lack confidence in our own abilities. Pam had always wanted to work in a beautiful historic building and was thrilled to secure a place at Snowshill Manor in the village of Broadway in the English Cotswolds. There was, however, a great deal to learn and it was important that she knew all the correct facts, figures and dates as part of her new job. She studied the information carefully, but still felt a little unsure of herself.

On her first day Pam was assigned one of the bedrooms in a part of the house that dated to the fifteenth century. Here, Pam was told to stand by a window with a lovely velvet window seat, which was roped off to visitors and from which point the whole room could be viewed. The windows were kept firmly closed because they were so fragile. While she was terrified of forgetting all the necessary information because of her nerves, Pam was thrilled to learn that this particular room had a reputation for being haunted. Standing in place, she steeled herself to greet an approaching group of visitors.

Just as Pam was getting ready to talk, she became aware of a commotion coming from another room and was called away to assist. There was an exhibition of Samurai armour in the next room and a large crowd of American tourists was eagerly asking questions, all at once it seemed! Having helped to meet this rush of enthusiasm Pam was relieved when the crowd moved on to another part of the building and she was able to return to her designated room.

Nerves still jangling, she walked to her spot by the window seat, saying a little silent prayer that she would get all the facts right. Stopping with a sigh in front of the window seat, she looked down and was amazed to find a huge white quill feather lying on the velvet seat! No window had been opened, of course, nor had a draft come from anywhere close by, and the feather was too big to have floated in from another room. It was safely tucked away from the public's reach behind the cord barrier. It was, however, placed where Pam could not possibly miss it and she felt a warm glow spread through her.

Pam knew that the angels were helping her, as they had many times before, and were communicating this to her with a very remarkable large feather.

✎ *Angel Top Tip* ✎

Self-belief and confidence are gained through actions. Behave as if you are more confident than you really feel. If you tell people that you're great, they might just believe you!

You are More Powerful than You Know

Like Pam in the last story, we are already more powerful than we know! Let's illustrate this with an example from everyday life: many people reading this book will use a computer every day. Both in the workplace and at home, computers have become a part of our daily routine upon which we have quickly become reliant. They are a modern-day marvel, making communication around the globe instantly possible. We are told, however, that most of us only use one per cent of our computer's capacity and all the other wonders it could perform remain a mystery to us. This is also true of many of us in relation to our own lives and potential. We are not even slightly stretched most of the time and there is so much more that we could give, enjoy and experience. Yet we are often held back by fear, lack of confidence and even lack of encouragement.

Take small steps in building your confidence; Rome was not built in a day and similarly you will not conquer your fears and misgivings overnight. Tell yourself each day: *I can do this and I will do this.* Just one little act that brings success will breed success. As your confidence in your abilities grows a little at a time, your self-belief will become stronger and stronger each day. Switch on the little star light inside, feel the glow and watch it grow bigger and brighter until you become a shooting star, shining for all to see. Stars and angels will light up your firmament – just give them and, most importantly, yourself a chance.

To aim for the stars, you first have to jump over the apple tree.

Dr Michael Williams

Divine Star

Believe the light of love will come through
others into your life, if you only allow it to.
If we love ourselves, we will love and trust
others. We shall then be drawn to others who
love and trust. In this way, we can establish a
flow and exchange of love.

EXERCISE:
Meet Your Inner Angel

Self-belief is a quality we develop as we grow in wisdom
throughout our lives. Earlier in this chapter, we discussed
Swedenborg's theory about our 'Inner Angel', which has all
the answers but which may communicate them to us in
many different ways. It may not necessarily make itself
known to us in the form of a guiding voice, but may make
us aware of its presence by a feeling, vision or even a fragrance. We can access this power to obtain the information
we need to make choices. Here are four keys to help you.

* Sit alone, at a time and place that will ensure no distractions. Feel what it is like to 'simply be'.

* Welcome your angelic guides, asking them to be with
you. Be patient and gradually become aware of any new
sensations you feel in your body.

* Open your mind to receiving messages and simply listen.

* Relax into a mindset of angelic energy by forgetting your
everyday distractions and opening yourself up to any

communication that your inner angel may have to offer you.

Be fully in tune with your spiritual essence,
sustained by a higher power.

Cherie Carter-Scott PhD
Life coach and motivational speaker

Angels Above and Below

As you become closer to the angelic presences in your life, you may feel inclined to share your good fortune with those around you, passing on to other people the kindness and companionship that the angels offer you.

Helping each other is a wonderful and wise way to gain insight and build self-belief. The old adage 'a trouble shared is a trouble halved' has a lot of wisdom. A good friend can be a co-counsellor, someone to talk to about our insecurities and fears. And a friend we can trust may well have his or her own problems to discuss, so the support is mutual.

Be kind to yourself and others in the knowledge that a good deed is never forgotten, not only by the person you help but by the Universe. What we give out comes back to us – sometimes a moment later, sometimes years later, but nevertheless it comes around.

EXERCISE:
Make Your Own Angel Cards

There are times when it feels especially good to know that we are part of a friendly, caring Universe. If you make your own set of angel cards you will be able to pick one whenever you want to be reminded of the angelic presence in your life.

You will need:

> A pen and a piece of paper
>
> A couple of sheets of thin white card
>
> A pair of scissors
>
> Some coloured pencils or felt-tip pens
>
> Decorative material such as glitter, tiny beads, scraps of material, feathers etc
>
> Your imagination

There are many packs of angel cards commercially available. But if you make your own your cards will be much more personal and special. First of all, give yourself permission to have fun! Now, sit down and think of ten positive qualities that you either possess and/or would like to possess, such as 'happiness', 'wisdom', 'courage', 'knowledge', 'spontaneity' etc. Write down a list of those qualities. Next to each quality, write down the name of a colour (or colours) that you think suits the quality.

* Cut 10 strips of card. Each strip should be roughly the same size, about 6 cm long by 2 cm wide.

* On each strip, write down the name of one of the qualities in your list. Use the colour pen that you chose for that quality. Leave a little room after the word, so that you can add some decoration.

* Draw a tiny angel in the space after the word. The angel can be a stickman with wings or as elaborate as you like, but try to make it reflect the quality of the word if you can. For example, if you have chosen the word 'happiness', your angel might be drawn in a yellow pen, wearing a bright smile and sprinkled with golden glitter. (If you don't want to draw an angel, your cards can be abstractly decorated with the materials that you have to hand.) Decorate all ten cards with angels and your materials.

* Put the cards in a place where you can easily draw upon them at random, whenever you feel in need of some inspiration. Alternatively, you can use them whenever you would like to meditate on a particular quality. And feel free to create more cards when you think of more qualities that you'd like to experience in your life!

Today is the First Day . . .

Living our lives is rather like weaving a blanket: all the events, people and situations are part of the pattern. How rich that pattern is depends on us individually. For instance, are we pursuing life, or is life pursuing us? Are we making things happen or waiting for things to happen to us? We comprehend the infinite only to the degree that we allow it to express itself through us, thus it becomes what we believe it to be.

Everyone is familiar with the expression 'today is the first day of the rest of your life'; we hear it so often perhaps we no longer realise just how true it is. Today is the perfect opportunity to create the life we want. We do not have to settle for what we have if what we have is making us unhappy. We can all create the changes we are looking for.

Give yourself permission to live life to the full, achieve

your potential and fly! You may have been struggling with financial problems; perhaps your relationships never seem to work, you have health issues or you are simply fearful of life itself. Whatever has been holding you back, make this the day that you decide to release the fear and not be influenced by others. Decide what it is you most want and ask for it, in the certainty that the Universe is a friendly place in which we are all supported in ways we can never have imagined. You too are always surrounded by love from the Divine and the angels, so choose to go forward in love and not backwards in fear. You already have all the power you need within, it just needs to be tapped and you will be astonished at its depth. Give yourself permission to live and be happy!

STAR POINTS TO PONDER:

I accentuate the positive.

I prioritise my goals in life.

I am more adventurous in daily life.

I will do one new thing each month.

I acknowledge my limitations to begin with and take small steps.

I forgive myself when I fail.

I am open to new opportunities.

2

The Star of Harmony

Oh thou art fairer than the evening air

Clad in the beauty of a thousand stars.

Christopher Marlowe
Dramatist and poet (1564–93)

Finding Balance

*H*armony is an important but often elusive quality in our lives. Most of us yearn for a more harmonious existence – one of balance, in which work and leisure, home comforts and nature, the needs of friends, family and our selves weave together into a seamless, happy whole without friction or discord. Nothing, however, is that simple.

Fortunately, there are some simple ways to bring a greater sense of harmony into your life. The practices and exercises in this chapter are designed to bring calm and clarity, so that the various aspects of your life will begin to gel.

As you will discover, it sometimes takes only slight adjustments to achieve a more harmonious lifestyle. And if you adjust your routine slowly, concentrating on one day at a time, the results can be spectacular.

You are a piece of the chain of light that is the Universe itself, therefore you are indeed a part of God.

Kryon

❧ *Angel Top Tip* ☙

Begin with a very small act. Look out of the window every day and take note of what you see there. If you learn to take inspiration from the beauty of nature all around you, you will be nurtured by nature herself.

Natural Harmony

People who live close to the land or who earn an income from working the land often live in harmony with nature in a way that town dwellers rarely experience. They have a particular awe and understanding of the elements; moments such as being caught outdoors in a blizzard, rescuing lambs in distress or being burned by the heat of summer sun remind them of how fragile life is and how swiftly the seasons pass. Despite the hardships of a life lived close to nature, such an existence also affords many opportunities for wonder and insight.

We both recall meeting a young man who declared that he could never live anywhere that was not surrounded by green hills and wide open spaces. The young man in question was fortunate enough to be able to live in just such a place; however, there are many city dwellers for whom this lifestyle is simply not an option, but they too may long for the harmony of the green hills. We townsfolk often have to work a good deal harder to let the harmony of nature and our daily lives combine.

If you cannot go to the countryside, why not bring it to you? Taking long walks in a country setting on a daily basis may simply not be possible, so ensuring we have enough personal space and time to ourselves is essential, as this enables us to connect with our inner thoughts and feelings. For natural inspiration, perhaps an interesting piece of driftwood placed on the hearth or a collection of pine cones or acorns in a decorative dish will bring nature closer to home. A colourful window box or a tub of flowers or shrubs placed at the front door will all help to bring nature into our lives.

There is a time for everything, and
a season for every activity under heaven.

Ecclesiastes 3:1

Divine Star

Find the opportunity to sit alone late on a warm summer night; you will visit a different world. There is enough magic out there for us all to fill our souls with natural harmony.

Reawakening Wonder

To experience the harmony of nature and our deep connection with it, we may have to reawaken the child-like sense of wonder that lies deep within. The link between children and nature is strong in many cultures, including in Haiti where trees are believed to protect children and are often referred to as their guardian angels. As children, many of us may have climbed trees or spent a holiday in the countryside or by the seashore, where we sensed the wonder in everything around us. The next time you visit the coast, observe any small child with a fishing net, dipping it into rock pools, and see the look of delight and amazement on that child's face when he or she finds some small marine creature. Children at the beach collect shells and stones, appreciating their beauty in a way that many adults have lost. Carter, the grandson of a friend of ours, keeps a collection of stones, pebbles and shells in a box, and refers to them as his 'treasures'. They truly are treasures, freely given by the earth for our appreciation.

Sadly, with the passing of the years we may forget how to engage with our surroundings; in many areas of our life, we 'unlearn' many aspects of wonder that we appreciated automatically as children. To reawaken your own inner child, give yourself the gift of time and treat yourself to a day in the country or by the sea. There, pause to draw strength from the everlasting nature of your surroundings. Be inspired. You may even sense the harmony at the heart of life that is all too often lost as we hurtle through our days, but which can be recaptured with only a little effort.

Holidays often afford a break from routine, enabling us to reclaim the wonderful feelings we had in our childhood and to revive the closeness we once felt to nature. Although some of us may not be able to indulge in a break away, we can nearly all make the effort simply to go for a walk in a local park or by a river bank. By marvelling at the very small things nature gives us, our hearts will fill with feelings of harmony, and life will be restored to balance. So find the time to simply stand and stare at the sheer beauty of the sea or sky. Emotions stirred by a wonderful sunset, seascape, rainbow, or the pattern in a puddle may bring your daily worries into perspective and help you to realise that there is indeed more to life than work and worries.

It is not healthy emotionally or mentally to stay rooted in the intellect only, disregarding the spiritual element in all around us. Most of us are aware in theory of spring with its uplifting beauty, the ways in which the summer sun brings colour to the earth, the glorious colours of autumn and the purity of winter white, but we may not appreciate the true extent to which the spiritual and natural are one. A feeling for the spiritual can connect us to surrounding beauty and vice versa, as great poets such as William Wordsworth (see below) and Coleridge knew.

Moreover, spiritual signs are all around us in nature, although most of the time we simply do not recognise them. Nature and angels are very close indeed, the natural world being used as a medium for their love. So if you listen closely to the world of nature and the Universe, you may discover that more spiritual experiences begin to come into your life.

. . . For I have learned

To look on nature, not as the hour

Of thoughtless youth, but hearing oftentimes,

The still sad music of humanity

Nor harsh or grating, though of ample power

To chasten and subdue. And I have felt

A presence that disturbs me with the joy

Of elevated thoughts; a sense sublime

Of something far more deeply interfused, . . .

William Wordsworth
Poet (1770–1850)

EXERCISE:
Recipe for Magic

Have you ever experienced tree magic? This little exercise may reward you with a sense of harmony with nature you never knew existed. The instructions and ingredients are simple: take one hot summer's day with a very blue sky. Unfold a blanket under the spreading arms of a large tree. Lie flat on your back and stare up through the leaves. It will take very little time at all before you will become mesmerised and filled with awe at such beauty.

The experience is very much like seeing a huge swathe of bluebells and feeling that emotional heady mix of the colour and fragrance – yet another instance of nature's harmony and magic. Likewise, watching waterfalls and chasing rainbows always promote inner feelings of harmony.

Written in Stone

A keen nature lover, Rebecca was rewarded with an angelic message that came to her in a particularly appropriate way.

It had been a stormy day in every sense for her. Her finances were at an all-time low and there was no sign of improvement on the horizon. The relatively new job that she had had such high hopes for was proving to be depressingly dull. However, as she lived in a small seaside town, jobs were at a premium and Rebecca knew there was little chance of change in that respect. Her personal life too was in the doldrums; having ended a recent relationship, she felt in her heart that she would be alone for ever.

The atmosphere in the cramped office had been uncomfortable and hostile that day, and Rebecca found herself watching the clock for home time. The leaden sky added to her dark mood as the rain lashed at the windows in heavy squalls. At last, the clock struck five and she was able to leave. After a meal in her little flat, she wondered what on earth to do next with her evening.

On impulse, she reached for her coat and made for the shore, instinctively feeling the need for fresh air both physically and mentally. It was early in spring, so the air was a little chilly. But at last the sky was blue, the storms of the day having finally passed. The sun was now shining on the sea. Walking along the beach, Rebecca felt her gloom starting to lift. Cheery people said hello as they walked their dogs, children with rosy cheeks were running on the sand, full of energy and laughter. Nature in all its beauty had touched her heart and she found herself picking up a shell or a stone here and there, and putting them into her pocket. When she at last arrived back home, a comforting warmth spread through her, as she realised how nature had given her the restorative balance she so badly needed that night.

Taking off her coat, she reached into the pockets and took out the shells and stones. Placing her treasures on the kitchen table, her attention was caught by one special stone. This was several inches in width and quite flat. As Rebecca looked at it she realised there was a series of lines embedded into its surface. All at once, she caught her breath, for there – plain as daylight – was the lined shape of an angel on the stone: a pale white line traced its head, body and wings distinctly against the surrounding dark grey.

Instantly, Rebecca knew this was a sign that her angel was reaching her through nature. Saying 'thank you' out loud, she felt in her heart that things would improve if she trusted her angel. And we are happy to report that indeed they did.

I arise today,

Through the strength of heaven,

Light of sun,

Radiance of moon,

Splendour of fire,

Speed of lightning,

Swiftness of wind,

Depth of sea,

Stability of Earth,

Firmness of rock.

Celtic affirmation

> ### ❧ *Angel Top Tip* ☙
>
> Look around. What do you see? How do your
> surroundings reflect your inner state? Do any
> signs or symbols catch your eye? What could
> you do to make your environment more
> harmonious?

How Colour Affects Our Lives

The seven-stranded rainbow is one of nature's strongest symbols of harmony. Ancient wisdom teaches that each colour in the rainbow relates to the mind and body in certain ways, with purple relating to the spiritual plane and red relating to the physical. Similarly, modern science has found that colour profoundly affects our emotions, and that yellow is the colour most likely to affect our moods.

Apparently the brain cannot differentiate between the yellow of sunshine and the yellow of cheerful paint; and yellow raises serotonin levels (the feelgood factor), which means it's a good idea to have yellow greet the eye first thing in the morning. A kitchen wall or hallway painted yellow will lift your spirits as you start the day.

Yellow mixed with red gives orange, an earthy colour whose name comes from Sanskrit. It is the colour of the early Church and symbolises fruitfulness. Orange is grounding and will help you to feel mellow.

But should your day include study or intellectual activity, then paint your study green. This colour reflects the calming influence of nature and is the most common colour chosen for places that may induce stress, such as hospitals and dental surgeries. Similarly, blue reduces blood pressure and will encourage a thoughtful atmosphere, whilst purple and lilac promote spiritual pursuits, as we have already seen.

Red, however, will raise your blood pressure, so large amounts of red in the home are not to be recommended. But touches of red may be energising – fast food outlets often feature red in their colour scheme because they want people to get up and go! Red promotes agitation and restlessness.

Making small adjustments in the palette of colours that you surround yourself with could help you in your pursuit of harmony.

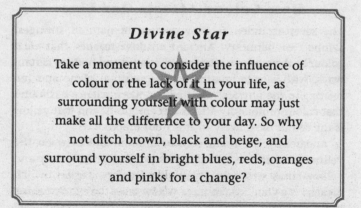

Divine Star

Take a moment to consider the influence of colour or the lack of it in your life, as surrounding yourself with colour may just make all the difference to your day. So why not ditch brown, black and beige, and surround yourself in bright blues, reds, oranges and pinks for a change?

Patsy's Painting

Without a shadow of a doubt, Patsy is one of the most colourful and cheerful people you could ever wish to meet. Not only is the glass always 'half full', but she is immensely grateful for having the glass in the first place! Extremely talented, Patsy excels as an artist, illustrator, writer and sculptress.

In recent years, Patsy has turned to angels for her inspiration. This change of direction has produced the most beautiful angel artwork. Many people reading this story will also be familiar with Patsy's hugely popular books for children, which have ecological messages and were written at an earlier time when Patsy had a demanding young family. Interestingly, several events and signs link that early period in her creative career to the present day, the first being a taped reading given to her by a friend who is gifted in the field of mediumship and clairvoyance. Amongst other things, her friend told Patsy that the time for her artwork to expand was not then, but would come at a certain point in the future.

The reading also confirmed that Patsy was very close to a particular grandmother, which might be considered an odd remark given that the grandmother in question had died before Patsy had even been born. However, this was indeed the case. A wonderful picture of Patsy's grandmother Sophia had always been prominent in the lounge of the family home when she was growing up, and as a young girl Patsy had felt drawn to it. Talking to this picture gave her comfort and confidence, accompanied by the certain feeling that her grandmother was listening. Family members would also tell Patsy that she resembled her grandmother in many ways.

More links with the past unfolded one autumn day in 2006 as Patsy lay ill in bed. Tom, Patsy's husband, arrived home and presented her with a copy of our newly published book *Angel Awakenings*, which perked her up considerably! The book fell open at a page relating the story of a young man who had visited the house of his recently deceased grandmother. He had not only seen the face of an angel at the upstairs window of her empty house, but had smelled the most wonderful fragrance on entering a room.

On reading this, Patsy realised that it had been a long time since she had 'chatted' to her grandmother's picture. On impulse she turned towards the picture of Sophia, now hanging on her bedroom wall, and talked to her about recent events. This brought such a feeling of peace and calm to Patsy that despite her illness she could not help but feel cheerful. It was then that it happened – the room filled with the most amazing fragrance, the likes of which Patsy had never smelled before. It was not a worldly perfume; that was for sure.

A little later Patsy replayed the tape that had been given to her by her clairvoyant friend many years earlier. Sheer astonishment was the most accurate description of her reaction, as she listened to the words spoken so long ago. Many events were happening as predicted: Patsy's work was coming to fruition and her career direction rapidly changing as new projects evolved. Signs, sensations and people were all entering her life as foretold; in fact, the various strands were all coming together in perfect harmony!

EXERCISE:
Recording Angelic Signs

You might be surprised by just how many signs, symbols and synchronicities there are in your own life, right now. To discover how the angels might be trying to communicate with you, start to observe the world around you on a regular basis and jot down your findings in the Angel Journal that you started for the Star of Self-Belief. Make a few notes on the following subjects:

1. The weather and the skies. Include your observations on the clouds and the stars, the sun and the phases of the moon (many diaries and calendars include the phases of the moon) and the patterns of rain, wind and shine. Also jot down your own moods and your thoughts about the behaviour of those around you. Do your feelings or the moods of your friends, family and colleagues seem linked in any way to the changing weather and skies?

2. Nature. (If you live in a built-up area, you may think that

this will be difficult, but even cities have parks and trees.) What plants are growing or dying? What are the birds, animals and insects up to? What can you see each day out of your window, either at home or work?

3. Coincidences and synchronicities. Has anything unusual happened this week? Make a note of any coincidences or anything slightly out of the ordinary that has taken place. Do these events seem linked in any way?

4. Look for possible threads of harmony or discord that thread their way through the days in each week. Do themes repeat themselves and do the events in your life connect with those in the natural world?

5. Jot down any angelic blessings, prayers or sayings that you would like to remember. Add clippings or cuttings that you find about angels. Make your journal a special place in which to record your thoughts about life and the gifts of the angels.

Everything in your life, every experience,

every relationship, is a mirror of the mental

pattern that's going on inside of you.

Louise L. Hay
Author and publisher

AFFIRMATION

Today, I invite harmony in all my relationships by speaking words that celebrate each moment.

Creating a Harmonious Environment

As you begin to become more aware of your external environment, you will become more attuned to the ways in which it reflects your inner landscape. Your thoughts and feelings may literally materialise as part of your surroundings. So it's high time for a little self-examination, and to ask yourself what it is exactly that is causing the lack of harmony in your life.

Perhaps you are spending far too much time on your work, staying later and later in order to get tasks completed? Yet deep down you probably know that leaving the office on time and enjoying some leisure hours will ensure that you will be fresh and energised on your return to work the next day. Or perhaps you are a slave to the house, unable to rest until every speck of dust is removed? But what about the cobwebs in your soul – they are far more in need of dusting. The house will need to be cleaned again and again, but cleanse your soul and you could feel the benefits for the rest of your life.

Could a lack of space literally and metaphorically be the problem? Holding on to articles that are no longer needed, and allowing them to build around you like a tortoise's shell, is tantamount to clinging onto old issues that hold you back. Clearing the decks will not only make your daily life easier, but will lift your soul and spring clean your mind as well.

Get rid of your clutter and replace it with a little luxury, perhaps by scheduling time for pampering yourself. Go on – you deserve it! Make the time to meet up with friends and laugh! The company of good friends has to be one of the best and quickest ways to restore harmony. Exercise your sense of humour and you may even be surprised to find that some of your most pressing problems can be viewed in a lighter spirit.

Cleaning the house while your kids are still growing is like shovelling the walk before it stops snowing.

Phyllis Diller
Comedian and actress

✎ *Angel Top Tip* ✎

Tell yourself daily that you are 'too blessed to be stressed'! Prioritise your tasks, focus on your to-do list and say to the angels out loud, 'I will bring harmony into my life and know for certain you will help me!'

Inner Harmony

As we have seen, harmony is truly present all around us; in the colours that surround us, the rhythms of nature and in the workings of the Universe; in the angelic signs, symbols and synchronicities that are sprinkled across our daily lives. However, it may be difficult for us to appreciate this if we are caught up in internal discord.

Take a moment to observe your thoughts and actions. Do they change from one moment to the next? In other words, is there a battle raging within you? You may be rocked by a fear that has its roots in the past and is making your present consciousness spin out of control into thoughts of scarcity.

Perhaps the single most important step in moving towards harmonious living is self-awareness. In other words, change your thoughts and you will change your world.

Remember: *we must always have a clear idea of what we desire.* Trust your consciousness and the power that is your consciousness. Whatever you need or desire as an individual, it is already a part of the main idea of the Universe. Trust, align and expect the angelic forces to demonstrate your spoken word.

Communicating with the angels is not something that is meted out to special people who have 'connected' with them or 'behaved' in a particular way. Your angels have been with you since you were born, patiently waiting for you to make your connection with them when you are ready. This guidance most often consists of impressions of energy that are felt, heard or sensed, and that are then translated into a form that is acceptable for each individual to accept in grace, love, harmony and humanity.

You may well ask how we can hope to bring peace, harmony and love into a planet blighted by war, poverty, terror and natural disasters. However, the angels understand this reality and your place in it.

Recognise when you are in balance,

you possess a level of strength and flexibility

that allows you to meet any challenge

effortlessly.

Deepak Chopra M.D.
Doctor and spiritual teacher

Angels of the Flame

Louise is an example of a down-to-earth person whose inner turmoil was finally resolved by trusting to a power higher than herself.

It had been fairly obvious why she couldn't sleep, as every time she closed her eyes she was tormented by thoughts of the project she was working on. Usually, she had great faith in her own judgement, but this time all reason appeared to have deserted her. Tossing and turning, she mulled over the concept she was trying to illustrate. Was her approach too complex, too technical or indeed too simple?

After several nights and days worrying about it, she decided to ask for help. Deciding to approach a much higher source than her work superior, she placed a candle on her bedroom windowsill and meditated for a while before asking her angel for a sign. Having no idea what this sign might be she nevertheless had great faith in the angels and immediately felt a sensation of calm engulf her. Blowing out the candle, she said her thanks and slept soundly that night.

Arriving at her place of work the following morning, she lifted down the file that contained all the notes for the troublesome project. Gazing at the file, Louise pondered once more: had she in fact 'got it right'? Taking a deep breath, she opened the file only to see to her astonishment a tiny, white, fluffy feather fall from it onto the carpet! There was no mistaking the sign – her angel had heard and answered her that all would be well. And it was.

Divine Star

There is a voice within every soul that guides
that soul through its lifetimes. This voice is
commonly referred to as intuition.

MEDITATION:

Tune into the Earth, Tune into the Stars

In order to tune into the harmony that surrounds us, such
as the harmony that can be found in nature, we often need
to free ourselves from internal discord. This meditation is
designed to help you tune into the natural harmony of the
Universe by letting go of any grievances that are holding
you back.

As you close your eyes, take a long, deep breath. Feel your
body relaxing as you continue to breathe slowly and deeply
. . . Breathing in . . . and breathing out . . .

Releasing any tension. Allowing passing thoughts to drift
away . . .

* Feel the golden energy of the Earth coming up through
  the soles of your feet, moving up through your entire
  body. Feel how this golden energy grounds you, creating
  a space of safety . . .

* Now feel light from the loving source of the Universe
  coming down through the top of your head, filling your
  entire body. See the colour of this light and know this is
  the perfect colour for you at this moment. Feel how light
  energy fills you with harmony and opens up all of your

inner wisdom. Bask in the moment of pulsing harmony; feel the energy in you vibrating, moving throughout your body. Allow the limitless, dancing energy to move out from you so that it surrounds you . . .

* In this space of harmony bring into your awareness someone in your life you feel victimised by in one way or another. Take a deep breath, and ask your Inner Wisdom to show you your role in creating a situation that has led you into a victim mentality. Watch without judgement as scenes flash before you. Take a moment now to feel whatever emotions have been sparked within you. Allow yourself to really experience these emotions.

* It's time now to let go of this victim mentality. Affirm that you are taking your power back and that you accept the role you played in creating the situation. Feel the chaos and heaviness of the past being released from you.

* In the newly created space, embrace your own power and your confidence in your ability to discern without assumptions. In this space of harmony, bring into your awareness a feeling of filling yourself with love for anyone you may have judged or been angry with. Now fill yourself with LOVE. Using the limitless loving energy you see around you, send this energy outward and into the Universe.

* Take a breath. In your mind's eye, place the person or situation in front of yourself. Let them or the situation know that you no longer choose to perceive yourself as a victim, that this situation no longer occupies a central place in your subconscious or life.

* Continue to send this affirming and empowering energy to the specific person or situation, or to the Universe in general until you feel complete and full. Feel yourself filling with love for this person or situation. Send love, trust and harmony towards this person or situation.

✳ When you feel complete, thank your guides for coming into your awareness and for the gift you have shared with them. Take a long, deep breath now . . . As you move out of this meditation, thank your body for its wisdom. And know that you will continue to carry this love, harmony, confidence, and clarity with you out into the world wherever you go today.

Divine Star

As we grow inside so we radiate a more positive personality. Those around us will respond in a more positive light and so the cycle begins.

Where Harmony Begins

No one is in control of your life except YOU. Therefore you have the power to change anything about yourself or your life that you want to change.

You can be the origin of all that you want to experience in your life, whether that is happiness, love, laughter, success or peace. If you have been caught in a vicious circle of negative thinking, of guilt, blame and shame, it's time to change your thoughts right now!

Can you recall a time in your life when you felt particularly happy? Do you remember an occasion when you felt the warm glow of success? It might have been a milestone event in your life, such as a graduation ceremony, a wedding or a promotion at work. It could also have been a simple everyday situation, such as finding an article you wanted in a shop, a wonderful evening with friends or even looking back to your childhood and an exciting event at school. Focus on this event, picture that happy self standing in front of you again, see your happy smile, and remember that sensation of a happy glow within. Hold tight to that image – it is where you are heading for once again.

Ask yourself, what would it take to become that person once more and experience those feelings of happiness again? Hold the thought for a few minutes and then make a list in your Angel Journal of what you really need to achieve in order to restore happiness and balance in your life. You will probably be surprised to find that your list is shorter than you had expected and that a lot of it is achievable. Keep that happy picture in front of you as a guiding light and act confidently in your determination to get there. Now it's time to work from the inside out, beginning by being honest with yourself and setting goals that are simple and achievable.

AFFIRMATION

Today, I am thankful to know the Inner Light is my source and supply.

EXERCISE:
Change with the Support of Your Angels

Change ultimately begins with you, but you don't have to go it completely alone. Although you may not always be aware of it, you will always have the support of the Universe and your angels whenever you wish to make a fresh start. This exercise is designed to help you make a conscious commitment to change.

Go to your point of quietness. Then invite your angels to stand behind you and become your creative partners as you begin to balance your life and energy.

* Create a wish list in your mind and convey this list to your guides, identifying the list as personal, professional, financial, emotional, mental or spiritual. Then, allow your angelic guides to lead you to the manifestation of your wish list. Beginners, trust this process!

* As you think about your goals and study the list in your mind's eye, look closely at yourself and your current relationships, and say out loud:

I am willing to change anything and everything about myself!

❧ *Angel Top Tip* ❧

Keep a glass bowl in the hall of your house and fill it with angel cards. Each morning before leaving home, choose a card to help concentrate your thoughts on the angels' message that day. You will start the day in the right frame of mind and have a head start on a stress-free day.

It's a funny thing about life;

if you refuse to accept anything but the best,

you very often get it.

Somerset Maugham
Novelist and playwright (1874–1965)

How Hannah Found her Angels

It seems that very often angels are encountered during the
most testing of times. For instance, we have heard stories
about angels stepping in to give comfort when grief becomes
too hard to bear. Similarly, dramatic rescues are another
common theme, as are tales of angelic guidance, when we
might be lost in every sense of the word. However, extreme
circumstances do not always have to be endured for a lucky
person to be blessed with a visit from the angelic realms.
Hannah is living proof of this. Here is her story, which begins
when she was a little girl of about four or five years old.

Living in the beautiful Cornish countryside with her
family, Hannah was fortunate enough to have a wonderful
landscape in which to roam, as well as breathtaking beaches
at her door. It was, she says, an idyllic life for a child. Her
memories of her childhood are all sunny; she and her family
were comfortable financially, and her parents provided for
them all in every way. An older brother and sister were much
adored by Hannah, whilst school, friends and activities all
ensured that her life could simply not have been happier.

One thing did puzzle Hannah, however. It was something
she couldn't explain and which was dismissed as 'daydream-
ing' by her mother. From time to time, Hannah would see
tiny bright specks of light in her bedroom, dancing around
her just before she went to sleep. They weren't threatening;
in fact, she felt a warm, happy glow whenever they appeared,

although she wished her mother could see them too. Her mother would merely say, 'Go to sleep, dear; it's just your imagination.'

Years passed and in time Hannah married and had a family of her own. She still lives in the area in which she grew up and she appreciates more than ever the wonderful scenery and wildlife outside her door.

One summer day last year, Hannah and her family decided to go on a picnic. Packing a hamper, they set off for a quiet beach not too far from their home. It was a wonderful day. Hannah and her husband played cricket with their two young sons; they swam in the clear water and thoroughly enjoyed their picnic.

Later that night, when the boys were in bed and her husband out attending a meeting, Hannah sat in her bedroom and thought about the day, her childhood and her life in general. She knew and appreciated just how fortunate she was, how much love had surrounded her from birth. Closing her eyes, she said out loud, 'God and your angels, I thank you for my many blessings. I promise that I shall look for ways of passing on my happiness to others not so blessed.'

Suddenly, warmth surrounded Hannah like the sun's glow and, as she opened her eyes, there were the little bright lights she recalled from her childhood dancing around the bedroom. She at once understood that the angels were communicating with her, joining in her happiness and good fortune, delighted in her appreciation of a life so blessed.

The greatest part of our happiness or misery depends on our dispositions and not on our circumstances.

Martha Washington
American First Lady (1731–1802)

AFFIRMATION

Today, I am joyous and I am loved.

Health and Harmony

Having engaged with our surroundings and taken positive steps to restore our inner equilibrium, we need to be sure that we are physically in harmony as well. Physical equipoise is needed for a well-rounded life, however much work we do on balancing our thoughts and feelings. As we will discover, learning to increase our energy levels will improve our general level of happiness and promote balance and harmony in other areas of our lives. Indeed, physical wellbeing supports mental health, and vice versa.

Whatever your starting point, whether you are a wheelchair user or already engage in some form of regular exercise, there will be something you can do to improve your sense of physical wellbeing. You might begin simply by becoming mindful of your posture, as improved posture may be instrumental in enhancing your health in many ways. You may find, for example, that the back pain you usually suffer from can be eliminated by following a few postural tips from the Alexander technique, and the accompanying sense of tension reduced.

Articles in magazines and newspapers often urge us to walk more, and they are absolutely right to do so. Today's world and the lifestyle it encourages, namely driving or riding everywhere, can lead to imbalances not only in the form of physical problems but in the guise of mental stress as well. Moreover, a lack of exercise in the fresh air can make us feel slightly depressed, whereas walking certainly encourages positive feelings and raises the spirits. The benefits of a walk often continue to be felt long after we have finished the exercise.

It's also well worth considering the benefits of such practices as T'ai chi, as the very nature of this ancient Chinese art is to promote balance and harmony. (Many of you will be familiar with the oriental concepts of yin and yang, which together form the black and white circle, and embody the meaning of the Universe in ancient Chinese philosophy.) The ancient Indian practice of yoga, with its emphasis on harmony between the mind and body, will also promote inner peace and balance.

The Universe totally supports every thought you choose to think, and to believe.

You have unlimited choices about what to think.

Choose balance, harmony and peace, and express it in your life.

Louise L. Hay
Author and publisher

The Melody of Life

So far we have talked about the harmony in nature, and the importance of nurturing a corresponding harmony in our thoughts and bodies, but we have yet to consider musical harmony. Having realised that the pitch of musical notes depends on the speed of their vibrations, the ancient Greek philosopher and mathematician Pythagoras also discovered that the planets move at different rates. He concluded that, as nature exists in harmony with itself, the planets must generate different sounds and create a 'harmony of the spheres'.

Whether or not the planets do generate a harmony of their own, music certainly brings magic into our lives, speaking to humans the world over without the need for words. Babies in the womb respond to music, and it can lift the spirits when we feel low. Music is a common everyday form of magic that manages to be unique at the same time, associated with the heavenly spheres and the angels themselves, who are often depicted in art playing musical instruments or singing.

*Sing like an angel
and the world will sing with you.*

Elizabeth Deane
Author

Musical Angels

How often, when we do a good deed for someone, will they respond by remarking, 'You're an angel'? Nurses are universally regarded as angels, as it takes angelic qualities for anyone in the caring professions to do a good job. However, occasionally we encounter people who we feel must actually be angels since they make such a difference to all those around them.

Two particularly amazing people work for an organisation in Manchester called 'Cancer Aid and Listening Line'. As the name implies, this organisation offers support to patients and their families in myriad ways. The charity's drop-in centres are especially valuable, offering advice, friendship, community spirit, relaxation treatments and entertainment to those in need. The manager of one such inspirational centre, and our first 'angel', is Janice Green. By organising these wonderful events and encouraging others to join in, she lights up the days of many with a serenity that rubs off on all around her.

Our second, very talented angel is Suzannah James, for whom the road that led to working in this field has been long and complicated. Suzannah was a highly successful professional singer in Europe. Frequent nominations for the BBC country music awards, such as Best Female Artist, as well as other events, led to Suzannah being invited to perform at the world-famous 'Blue Bird Café' in Nashville, Tennessee, where she gained a reputation as a successful 'New Country' singer, writing and performing with prominent artists such as Bob Welch of Fleetwood Mac. Throughout all these years there was, however, a feeling of unease which Suzannah found hard to identify. In spite of her success, she was aware deep inside that she was somehow on the wrong path. Almost subconsciously, she felt she was being called to another life altogether.

Leaving Nashville and the country scene behind, Suzannah returned to England. There, she found herself involved in a series of events that in retrospect seem to have been angelically influenced and which led to her working as a volunteer at St Anne's Hospice. She had indeed discovered her true vocation, finding the work rewarding and fulfilling on many levels.

It was not long, however, before her musical talents came once more to the fore and Suzannah found herself performing for the people in the support groups – to their immense delight. Her musical composition took on a very different complexion and she found herself composing songs with a spiritual element, especially angel-themed songs. After reading one of Glennyce's books, *Teen Angel*, she put one of the inspirational stories to music and the lovely CD *Teen Angel* was created.

Her next step was almost inevitable: leading singing workshops for the people attending the cancer aid groups. These proved to be hugely popular. One day this led to the writing of a song by one of the groups. Each person wrote a few lines describing the moment. Emotions were high as some people wrote about family and friends no longer with them, or the journey they themselves were taking, leaving loved ones behind.

Suzannah took the group's contributions home with her and began to work on the project of putting their thoughts to music. Eventually, the beautiful song 'Shine: Always and Forever' was formed. A talented musician, Pete Newton, who just happened to be Suzannah's son, begged and borrowed recording equipment and the song was at last recorded on CD.

With the Christmas party fast approaching, Suzannah and Pete worked hard to get the song ready to perform for the group as a surprise. When played for them, the song was so beautiful that many group members found themselves in tears, saying that the very notes seemed to fall from the realms of the angels.

One special member of this group, Frank, had contributed lines to the song and dedicated them to his wife, who he knew he would have to leave behind in a very short time. Frank was very poorly that day but was determined to attend the Christmas party to hear the song. And hearing it left him thrilled and happy, even though he was so terribly ill. Courageously, he gave a final speech at the party and died only a few days later.

The group claims that this is probably the first pop song to be written by a group of forty- to ninety-year-olds! And a recording of it is to be sold to raise funds for the organisation. Here are a couple of the verses:

Shine: Always and Forever

Tender nights as shadows fall,

I close my searching eyes,

Sleep covers me and silently I dream,

Of you, so close so real.

Shine, always and forever, please believe for me,

If my faith should fail

Shine, always and forever, please believe for me

Send angels to guide me, shine.

**(Verses composed by members of Cancer Aid and
Listening Line, Manchester.)**

It is a beautiful, uplifting song and once more Suzannah has
found that the media are interested in her work. She has, in a
way, come full circle, but this time the song in her heart is
inspired by the angels – a truly heavenly harmony.

*Angels are reassurance that the supernatural
and the realm of God are real.*

Richard Woods

A Harmonious End

Our basic need for harmony is often as applicable in death as it is in life. Recent statistics reveal that more and more of us are requesting a 'woodland burial'. We wish our last resting places to be amongst green fields with perhaps a tree planted at our heads instead of a large stone memorial. Coffins made from basket weave or strong cardboard are ecologically friendly options, ensuring harmony with nature in death, allowing us to take our leave with as little baggage as when we first entered the world.

By ensuring that we tie up loose ends, resolve our differences, and make peace with those we have hurt or kept at a distance, we will be on track to end our days harmoniously in spirit as well as body.

❧ *Angel Top Tip* ❧

Remember, we are all in this together: harmony is the goal of everyone. To experience harmony in your life, start by creating a more harmonious relationship with those closest to you. Then spread this into the wider reaches of your life. Let the light of harmony shine for all to see.

A Resting Place

Wendy is a close friend of ours who found herself having to make funeral arrangements at a particularly difficult time. Life had been a struggle for her for a while as she tried to come to terms with the fact that her mother was terminally ill. Finally, in the week before Christmas 2006 her mother died. Christmas is always an extremely emotional time of the year in which to lose a loved one, but adding to Wendy's distress was the possibility that the funeral might have to be postponed until after the Christmas period.

Firmly believing in angels and expecting to receive their help, Wendy asked that this potential problem might be resolved. Knowing also that her mother's last wishes were to be buried somewhere green and pleasant, Wendy asked for help with this too. At the very last moment, everything fell into place. The kindly vicar of a beautiful old country church agreed to hold the funeral service immediately before Christmas and secure a lovely resting place for Wendy's mother in the grounds.

The day of the funeral service dawned, but the country was shrouded in thick fog. It was so bad that planes were grounded at airports all over the United Kingdom and scenes of chaos ensued on the roads. This was certainly not the calm and lovely day that Wendy had envisaged. At the close of the service, everyone prepared to walk into the little graveyard for the interment. As they approached the plot, something amazing happened. The fog swiftly cleared, the sky turned deep blue and the sun began to shine. Slowly the coffin was lowered and at that very moment the birds began to sing loudly. Local farm animals joined in the chorus and all nature seemed to be in harmony at that precious moment. Wendy knows the angels had responded to her pleas and rewarded her belief. She had indeed believed and received.

*In you is all of heaven. Every leaf that falls is
given life in you.*

Each bird that ever sang will sing again in you.

*And every flower that ever bloomed has saved
its perfume and its loveliness for you.*

A Course in Miracles

Divine Star

Picture your very own Angel of Harmony,
serene of face and radiating calm. Know that
she is there for you to guide you whenever life
gets frenetic.

Harmony Forever

The Star of Harmony is a continual presence throughout our
lives. It accompanies us from the cradle to the grave, making
its presence felt in the beauty of the world around us, in the
sounds we hear, through the very movements of the planets.
And yet so often we spend our days searching for it, we fear
that we don't possess it or we live our lives in such a way that
harmony seems impossible for us.

Often, we simply need to slow down and open our eyes to
the wonder all around, to raise our energy levels by taking
care of ourselves physically and mentally, and to nurture our
personal happiness by tuning into our hearts. If we listen
carefully, if we look again at the amazing patterns and syn-

chronicities that surround us, we will sense what has always been there – our natural birthright, the Star of Harmony, shining down on us.

STAR POINTS TO PONDER:

I am going to take time out to be me.

I believe in the harmony and support of the Universe.

I listen to music that lifts my spirits.

I spend quality time with those I love.

I take time to appreciate the natural world.

I care for my body as well as my mind.

I appreciate the connections between things.

3

The Star of Gratitude

Each day accept everything that comes to you as a gift. At night, mentally give it all back. In this way, you become free. No one can ever take anything away from you for nothing is yours.

Daniel Levin
Author

Taking Stock

The Star of Gratitude is all about counting our blessings, which is not always easy, we know. We may feel that we are going through life stumbling from one crisis to another; that unhappiness has become a way of existence for us and we are caught in a negative spiral. The more miserable we feel, the more convinced we are that it will always be so. At this point, the whole situation may indeed become worse, as often the more miserable we are the more misery seems to come our way. We are all attracted to warm, generous people, such as friends who make us laugh and who look on the bright side, literally cheering our day. But what about those people who, the corners of their mouths pointing downwards, complain, 'Oh dear, everything happens to me'? Of course it does, because they set themselves up for disappointment and sadness. Theirs is a self-fulfilling prophecy as their pessimistic outlook attracts negative results in all they do.

However, if we begin to take stock of our experiences at the end of each day and consciously look for a positive, happy element – just one – then that will be a start. So how about your own day so far . . . perhaps you found a bargain in a shop? Has a small child smiled at you? Did you see a rainbow? Did you notice the fresh shoots pushing through the soil or did you eat a delicious piece of cake? These may appear to be small blessings but if you begin to concentrate upon them you will soon find that you start consciously and unconsciously looking for others the following day.

Take stock of every small pleasure that comes your way on a daily basis and your blessings will become more obvious to you and may even seem more frequent. Like most things in life, practice makes perfect. If we deliberately close our eyes to the blessings around us, they will disappear from view, but gratitude for them will automatically bring an abundance of them into our lives.

You and your unhappiness are not one and the same being; you can turn your life around by using the many talents that are already within you – you just have to winkle those talents out, which we will help you to do in this chapter. So give your inner eyes a good rub, look around you and count the many blessings that are certainly yours, and give thanks!

*If the only prayer you say in your life
is 'thank you' that would suffice.*

Meister Eckhart
Theologian and Mystic (1260–1328)

> ❧ *Angel Top Tip* ❧
>
> Gratitude for this moment is the element that
> shifts us into acceptance of what we are
> actually experiencing right now.

Dutch Courage

Counting our blessings can sometimes turn a potential disaster into a triumph! Let Glennyce tell you about the time she was about to embark upon a short trip to the city of Amsterdam:

We had been looking forward to this trip for months; it was to be a 'women's week' and our group of six friends planned to visit art galleries, take a boat along the canals, go shopping and enjoy each other's company. The day arrived and we met at Liverpool airport, eager to set off. Our flight was called and we all made our way to the departure desk brandishing our passports.

At the gate, the first friend to show her passport was told by a very stern-looking gentleman that it was out of date and she wouldn't be flying anywhere that day. How we laughed – this was Liverpool after all, known for the wit of its people. However, it was no joke: the poor woman hadn't noticed that her passport was indeed out of date. A black cloud descended over the group. 'You must go ahead with the trip,' our friend said firmly. 'Don't worry, I shall think of something.'

We couldn't imagine what she might think of to make the situation better, so with heavy hearts we boarded our plane. Arriving in Amsterdam we were pleased to find that our hotel was very central, and that it was absolutely delightful, full of character. Trying hard to enjoy the prospect of exploring the city, we nevertheless missed our friend terribly.

The following morning, as we entered the dining room for an early breakfast, we were astonished to see our friend walk into the room with a large grin on her face. She explained that, on leaving us, she had jumped into a taxi that had taken her into Liverpool, where she had waited at the passport office while they renewed her passport. Then she had booked into a luxury hotel for the night and caught the first flight to Amsterdam that morning. She declared that a night of luxury and pampering was good for the soul; that she was only half a day late and now she was raring to see the sights!

What a wonderful attitude she had; several of our party declared that they would simply have gone home and moped, feeling sorry for themselves at missing a holiday. One friend said she would simply have sat down and cried with frustration. Turning what might have been a disaster into a time of fun showed real talent; in fact she had even added pleasure to the trip. And we were all grateful to our friend for being so resourceful and restoring our happiness.

Reality is something you rise above.

Liza Minnelli
Actress and singer

Divine Star

An attitude of gratitude prepares our consciousness to be receptive to our desires.

We Are All Worthy

Using time wisely to turn what might be a disastrous situation into a triumph takes courage, but if we practise focusing with gratitude on what we have instead of bemoaning what we have not, we can all turn our lives around.

Time itself is a precious gift. Yet so many of us complain about having 'no time' or 'too little time' instead of being grateful for what we do have. Indeed, many of us would be surprised if we realised exactly how much free time we have at our disposal. Yet how often have we refused invitations or failed to join an interesting activity because we 'don't have enough time'? What we really mean is that we have a martyr attitude, and may be driven by an unnecessary sense of duty. We should actually say a polite 'no' to some of the tasks we just think we should be doing.

Today's world offers us a huge variety of leisure activities to choose from, and if we manage our lives so that we can include some of these we will feel our spirits lift and happiness creep back into our lives. We are all worthy of time for ourselves. So make a deliberate effort to schedule 'me time' into your life, as it will enrich all areas of your existence. And give thanks for all your opportunities and embrace them.

Just for today, I will have a quiet half-hour all by myself, and relax.

During this half-hour, some time, I will try to get a better perspective on my life.

Kenneth L. Holmes
Author

AFFIRMATION

Today, I choose to make all things new.
I am grateful for my ability to release
the past and create an incredible life.

Gratitude is Everything

We sometimes get stuck in worry whenever we focus on worry itself. We may have been inadvertently taught to do this by people who believe that if we look hard enough at a problem, we'll eventually figure it out. But if we focus on an individual problem while we ourselves are full of problematic feelings, the problem itself may simply expand – the situation may seem worse than it really is.

On these occasions we must shift this energy so that we find ourselves in a state of total gratitude and grace. We must take responsibility for our selves, our actions and our choices in life. When we each stand firm in our life choices without judging others, it is then that we become empowered creators and then that we inspire others to trust their own choices. Life is a work in progress and each moment we have the choice to be renewed, refreshed and ready to move forward in the presence of each other. All choices are perfect, as the Archangelic realm reminds us so often.

So do we simply disregard our worries and fears? No, for they too are a part of us. We glance at them, long enough to register where to do our work in consciousness around the problem and especially towards the solution. The journey towards true soul freedom and success begins with looking at self. This realisation helps us move to a bigger picture of life, in which we see ourselves as we really are: we see our angelic guides, and we recognise our oneness with the Universe.

We must stand firm in gratitude and not surrender to

doubt or fear. This simple act will help us to open our conscious connections to our soul's love, where we will find the reassurance that allows us to let new things and conditions come into our lives.

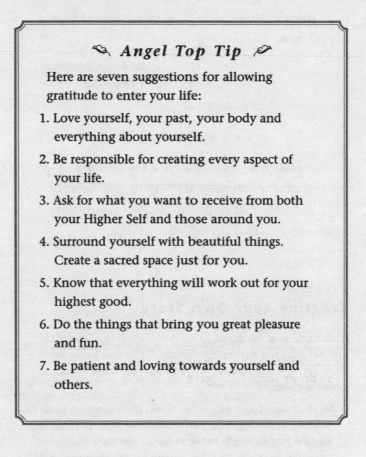

❧ *Angel Top Tip* ❧

Here are seven suggestions for allowing gratitude to enter your life:

1. Love yourself, your past, your body and everything about yourself.

2. Be responsible for creating every aspect of your life.

3. Ask for what you want to receive from both your Higher Self and those around you.

4. Surround yourself with beautiful things. Create a sacred space just for you.

5. Know that everything will work out for your highest good.

6. Do the things that bring you great pleasure and fun.

7. Be patient and loving towards yourself and others.

Asking is the beginning of receiving.

Through a simple believing prayer,

you can change your future,

you can change what happens one minute from
now.

Dr Bruce Wilkinson
Theologian and author

AFFIRMATION

Today, I greet change as a welcomed
friend. I am now willing to release any
fear, so that new things and conditions
can come into my life.

EXERCISE:
Creating Your Own Story

This exercise is designed to help you explore some of the themes that run through your life. Once you know what they are, you can look at ways to address them and create positive change.

1. In your Angel Journal, write down the names of some of your favourite legends, fairy tales and stories. What themes run through those stories – are they about vanquishing dragons, rescuing maidens, overcoming obstacles? Notice if these stories reflect any important values or ideals in your own belief system.

2. List any seven challenges you are facing at this time.

3. List any seven frustrations that you are experiencing at this time.

4. List seven happy memories.

5. List seven things that have made you smile this week.

6. List seven wishes for the future.

7. Write a short version of one of the favourite stories that you picked, but incorporate some of the challenges, frustrations, memories and wishes that you have uncovered. Create solutions for the problems. How does your new version differ from the traditional story?

We can all rework the stories of our lives, although it may take some imagination and determination to give them happy endings.

Here Comes the Sun

Kelly's story shows how angels can help us to move on and emerge from sadness into a glorious new future. And, even more wonderfully, the very way in which Kelly's story came to me (Glennyce) shows that the angels may be closer to us than we realise:

The day was cold and frosty with a hint of snow yet to come. The weather forecast promised a little sun later in the day, but I felt they were being overly optimistic. Taking a break from writing this book, I went to the kitchen to make a coffee. Sipping the hot drink, I stared through the window and found myself saying silently, 'I could use a little sunshine please.' I was not at all sure whom I was addressing but the angels must have heard me, because when I returned to my computer and checked my emails, there was a message that filled me with sunshine.

Kelly had read one of my books and was writing to tell me about something that happened when she was younger. She explained that some years ago her whole family had suffered a terrible loss with the death of a dear friend. The friend had died only two days before Kelly's birthday, which felt like additional sadness. This particular evening, Kelly was alone in the house and the sensation of grief was overpowering. Longing for comfort, she went and snuggled down in her mother's bed, wanting to feel close to her.

Looking up suddenly, she gave a gasp. There in the corner of the bedroom was an astonishing sight. A huge angel stood there, a truly breathtaking sight. Kelly described the figure as being at least eight feet tall, with shoulder-length hair, hands held in a prayer position and head tilted slightly to one side. The figure was shining and golden, radiating a warm sensation that filled Kelly's heart.

Years later, when Kelly recalls the experience, she feels that incredible warmth again. The whole episode lasted only a few moments but Kelly says it will stay with her a lifetime. As a child, Kelly had been rather fearful, a feeling that often crept back into her daily life. However, after she saw the angel all fear left her and she found her life changing. In her own words: 'The angel gave me something that changed my heart and soul, a reassurance that will stay with me always.'

Life completely changed direction for Kelly, as exciting opportunities to travel emerged and literally broadened her horizons. A talented artist, she realised her dream of a university education.

'Truly,' says Kelly today, 'I could not have achieved so many things in my life, had it not been for the wonderful angel that night.' Kelly's heart is not only full of love and warmth, but profound gratitude.

EXERCISE:
Uncovering Your Hidden Talents . . .

Although not all of us are as fortunate as Kelly to have a life-changing angelic encounter, we each of us have inner talents we can express.

* To discover your hidden talents think back to your childhood. What activities did you particularly enjoy when you were little? Did you like drawing, acting, repairing broken bikes or was there something else that gave you pleasure?

* If you hear of another person's success in a particular field, do you ever feel envious or think 'I could have done that'? If so, what activity is it? Why do you think that person has been successful and why do you think you respond so strongly to their success? What is stopping you from having a go?

* What gives you a sense of fulfilment in your life now? How can you make this activity a greater part of your routine? Could you join a class or a course, or simply practise it once a week? What steps can you take? Maybe there is an activity you always longed to participate in and never summoned up the courage to try?

* Now is the time to discover your personal areas of unplumbed happiness. Feel grateful for the pleasure this discovery will bring you, and it will bring you much pleasure, be assured. Don't worry if you discover that you aren't outstandingly gifted in your chosen field; give yourself permission to have fun and spread the happiness around.

Life has more than its share of responsibilities and worry. Make a concerted effort to connect with the 'real' you and to work with the considerable blessings you already possess. Discover the gifts and talents that you really have, but that might have been hidden away from view.

❧ *Angel Top Tip* ❧

It is important to find the time for a little light relief and to share the gift of laughter through activities that you enjoy. Like everything else in life, the more you practise the better you become, so 'give the giggle a go'; it can only make life better. The healing power of laughter will light up your life and make you feel better on a physical level too. Work freely with the power of laughter and its healing properties.

We all have tests in life.
Love and the angels will help us pass.

Richard H. Lucas
Author

MEDITATION:
Walking the Path of Gratitude

This meditation will help you to leave behind the various thoughts and emotions that have been obstacles in your way, and to make your way towards a brighter, more carefree future.

As you close your eyes, take a long . . . deep . . . breath. Feel your body relaxing as you continue to breathe slowly and deeply. Breathing in, and breathing out . . . Release any tension. Allow passing thoughts to drift away.

* See yourself outside in a beautiful open space. In this space of complete relaxation and peace, bring into your awareness a situation in your life that has been troubling you.

* Notice now that you are standing at the fork of a path in your endless outside space.

As you turn your head to look behind you, from where you came, notice that the path you have been on was rocky. Recognise this path as the path of fear in relation to the situation in your life you have brought into your awareness.

* Notice all the obstacles on that path, all the hurdles and roadblocks. Notice how unstable and lacking in support that path was . . . How narrow it was . . . Thank your inner wisdom for bringing you to the fork in the path you have now arrived at.

* As you face forward again, notice the two paths in front of you. One is a continuation of the rocky path you were on before, the path of fear. The other is a much wider, smoother path. You recognise it as the path of gratitude.

* Take a deep breath now and affirm to the Universe your choice to go forward on the path of gratitude. With the situation in your life at the forefront of your awareness, begin moving forward on the path of gratitude spread out before you.

* Notice how you glide, how supported you feel – as if there is energy helping you along, assisting you. Notice how wide the path is, how much space it provides you.

Feel the ease with which you move along this pathway of gratitude. See how any obstacles or roadblocks simply fade into nothingness.

* Sense all of the loving guidance of the Universe walking right along with you. Feel the gratitude moving through-

out your body, the freedom of release. Embrace the love and support you are feeling . . .

* Take a deep breath now and as you move out of this meditation, affirm your gratitude, the essence which you have created.

The Kindness of Strangers

If you try to change direction and make your way towards a more fulfilling future, grateful for all that you have received and that you will receive, you can rest assured that you will always have the support of the angels. The Universe wants what is best for you and will give you the support you need. However, sometimes that support may manifest itself in surprising ways.

Many stories reach us about people being helped suddenly by perfectly ordinary-looking strangers in everyday dress. These strangers often appear swiftly, as if from thin air, and disappear equally quickly. The statement 'I turned to thank them and they had completely vanished' is pretty much common to all the accounts.

From the evidence we have collected, it would seem that everyday angels are amongst us all the time, appearing in whatever form is least alarming and most suitable for the circumstances. We have heard many times of those who have been helped in public places, such as on trains or at airports, and who receive the help they require without attracting attention. It would appear that angels are good at adapting to the modern world, helping swiftly and unobtrusively in our lives, as will be apparent in our next story about Norma.

All God's angels come to us disguised.

James Russell Lowell
Poet, critic and abolitionist (1782–1861)

An Angel in Disguise

Have you ever wondered how you would react in an emergency? Most of us hope that we would take swift and effective action, doing all the right things in all the right order. The truth is, however, that many of us would simply be frozen to the spot with shock or panic.

As a young girl of just ten years old, Norma was to discover for herself how terrifying an emergency situation could be. That particular day, Norma had been left in charge of the house and her younger brother, so she was feeling very grown up and responsible. It was an extremely hot summer's day and all the windows in the house were wide open, including the one in the kitchen. Norma decided to make a cup of tea and turned on one of the gas rings on top of the cooker, which was situated directly beneath the open kitchen window. A sudden gust of wind blew the kitchen curtains across the top of the cooker, where they caught light. In an instant the curtains were completely on fire and Norma gasped in horror as the flames spread quickly upwards. She felt herself shaking in fear as she attempted to throw water on the flames with a small jug, but that proved ineffective and she was horrified at the situation she found herself in.

It was at this precise moment that terror rooted her to the spot and she found she was incapable of moving a muscle. Her mind was a complete blank as to what she should do next; she could only stare open-mouthed at the scene unfolding before her. To her astonishment, at this moment a tall man in a navy blue uniform appeared behind her and swiftly moved towards the sink. He took the large, full bowl of water sitting there and threw it at the curtains in one mighty swoop. Amazingly, as quickly as it had started the blaze was gone, extinguished instantly.

Norma stood in stunned silence for a moment. Then, remembering her manners, she stirred herself to say a huge thank-you to the stranger. However, there was no one in the kitchen save herself! The man in uniform seemed to have disappeared as quickly as the flames and must have left the kitchen without a word.

Impossible, she thought – he would have had to open the kitchen door before leaving the room. Reasoning that the man had exited into the street, she ran after him, determined to express her gratitude. But there was no one in view; the street was totally empty of people in both directions.

It occurred to Norma that the man's uniform might have been that of a tram operator; the tram stopped just around the corner from her house. Dashing around the corner, she fully expected him to be in his tram ready to move away. However, there was no tram in sight as far as the eye could see.

To this day Norma often contemplates this incident, mulling it over in her mind, but she has never been able to find a rational explanation. At the time, she had so much wanted to thank the stranger for saving her house and possibly her life. Now she wonders if he might have been an angel of some description. Had she been helped out of a frightening and dangerous situation by some sort of spiritual guardian?

AFFIRMATION

Today, I give thanks for everything. I am joyful in my gratitude and blessings.

Angel Encounters

There is a common denominator in the angel stories that involve young people such as Norma, and it is that even many years later those involved always recall the events as clearly as if they had happened only the previous day. Other childhood memories may fade, but these angelic encounters stay crystal-clear for ever.

When it comes to such encounters, it often seems that we try to search for the logical explanations when there simply is no logic in the situation at all. No matter how hard we may try, the whole incident appears to have only a mystical explanation and we are forced to trust the angels. Interestingly enough, when we do just that, it appears that the angels will intervene even more readily. We need to learn to suspend our disbelief. The following story is an example of another angelic rescue that defies explanation.

Rescue on the Emerald Isle

For as long as anyone in the family could remember, Colin and Sarah had talked about visiting Ireland. Each year they would contemplate the trip but somehow it never actually happened. Now here they were at long last, finally preparing in earnest for their Irish holiday. Their children teased them and said they would only actually believe it was going ahead when Colin and Sarah had landed in Ireland. Laughing and waving cheerily, the couple left for the airport, knowing that their children were now old enough to take care of themselves in their absence.

The flight was smooth and comfortable, and the hire car was waiting for them at the airport as arranged. Colin and Sarah had three glorious weeks ahead of them in which they intended to see as much of the country as possible. Full of anticipation and excitement, they arrived at their first night's accommodation. That evening, they studied maps and chatted to the hotel manager about interesting places to visit, explaining that they intended to explore the beautiful countryside. With plans in place, they set off the following morning. Several days unfolded in sheer pleasure; the holiday was everything they had hoped it would be and all their expectations were fulfilled.

It was in the middle of the second week that problems arose. Driving along a mountain road in what appeared to be the middle of nowhere, the car started to play up, making very unnerving noises, and finally it juddered to a halt. Colin jumped out to look under the bonnet, although as Sarah was well aware he didn't have a clue what to look for! Never mechanically minded at the best of times, he was at a total loss with this unfamiliar make of car. In the event, no amount of staring at the engine made the slightest bit of difference. They were well and truly stranded, and, looking out from their high vantage point, they could see that the road ahead and behind them was completely empty in both directions.

'Oh well, someone is sure to come along shortly,' they told themselves, but in fact no one did. To make matters worse, it began to rain for the first time since they arrived in Ireland and the whole outlook turned very gloomy indeed.

Suddenly, as if from nowhere, a bright red car appeared. They could not understand why they hadn't seen it in the distance. The car came to a halt behind Colin and Sarah's vehicle and two men climbed out. Smiling broadly, they came over and asked if the couple needed help. Hugely relieved, Colin answered that indeed they did, he was totally useless mechanically! In what appeared to be only five minutes, the men had started the car. Then, without another word, they jumped back into their own vehicle and drove away. Colin shouted 'Thanks!' at them as they roared off.

Turning to Sarah, he said, 'What amazing luck to have those two stop and help.' As he looked back at the road only seconds later, he was astonished to see there was no sign of the red car anywhere. 'Impossible,' Colin thought, 'I can see the road ahead for miles as it winds around the mountain; they couldn't possibly have vanished from view in only a couple of seconds!' In sheer disbelief he continued to stare and shake his head.

Sarah, however, said that she had read a similar story in a book about angels and perhaps the two men were angels in everyday dress. 'Normally,' Colin said, 'I would have laughed heartily at that statement, but today I'm prepared to believe they may just have been heavenly helpers.'

Sarah agreed. 'As unlikely as it may sound when we tell other people,' she said, 'I firmly believe we had an angelic experience.'

'Well, one thing is for sure,' Colin replied, 'we're truly grateful.'

Count your blessings.
A grateful heart attracts
more joy, love and prosperity.

Cheryl Richardson
Personal coach, lecturer and author

Spread a little Happiness

One of the truest sayings we have heard is 'what goes around comes around', which is certainly true of gratitude: the more we show to others, the more gratitude will be sent our way. Likewise, small acts of kindness spread happiness. If we do little favours or behave well towards others, it doesn't generally take long for the happiness to come right back to us.

Gratitude is contagious; it creates a warm, glowing feeling that spreads like sunshine, encouraging growth and abundance. Simply thanking the angels for help and guidance will bring more help and guidance into your life. Similarly, if you see the good and the blessings in all around you, this attitude will rub off on all you meet. Soon the warm feeling will spread like jam and prove to be just as sticky!

Express your own gratitude today. Tell a friend how grateful you are for her friendship and perhaps treat her to lunch or a trip to the cinema. Give your window cleaner a cup of coffee and a piece of cake, and thank him for doing such a good job. Your windows will sparkle like diamonds ever after! Thank your taxi driver for getting you safe and sound to your destination, complimenting him on his driving skills: the warm feeling will spread to all who ride in his taxi that day.

In her book *Life Makeovers* Cheryl Richardson encourages us to send small thank-you gifts to those who least expect them. She suggests taking an apple pie to the local Salvation Army hostel – for the staff, not the residents, to thank them for the wonderful work they do. This is a lovely way of saying thank-you to a whole section of the community.

The small things you do every day – smiling at a stranger or paying someone a compliment – bring you closer to your spiritual truth, the purity of your soul.

Deepak Chopra M.D.
Doctor and spiritual teacher

Divine Star

Living a spiritual life in the world today means
that, if we are to remain spiritually healthy, as
we receive so must we give.

EXERCISE:
Express More Gratitude in Your Life

1. Write down the names of five people who are important
   in your life. Next to each name, write a short sentence
   that sums up why you appreciate that person. Choose
   one of the people from your list. Sit down and write a
   letter to that person, explaining why he or she is so
   important to you, what special qualities that person has,
   and why you are grateful he or she is in your life. Explain
   in what ways you think the world is a better place
   because of that person. Now, it's up to you: you can simply throw the letter away or keep it in a special place,
   perhaps in your Angel Journal. Or you can pluck up your
   courage and send it to the person you addressed it to. It
   might make their day.

2. Make a list of the things you are most grateful for in your
   life. Put one copy in your wallet, one on the refrigerator,
   and one by your bed. Whenever you feel negative or
   depressed, take out the list and read it.

3. Create a Gratitude Log. Keep your Angel Journal by your
   bed, and every night before you go to sleep write down
   three things you are grateful for that day.

4. Practise telling at least one person a day something you
   are grateful to them for.

5. Write yourself a Gratitude Letter, thanking yourself for all your hard work in this book, and telling your Inner Child how proud you are of all the growth and healing that has taken place.

Make gratitude part of your daily routine. If you appreciate each little thing that comes your way, imagine how much easier it will be to appreciate the wonder of your life as a whole when you look back over the years.

All-Enveloping Love

When telling her story, Marie emphasised the fact that she is a life-long committed Catholic and has had a profound belief in angels right from the cradle. Each day of her life she has said a little prayer to her guardian angel, asking for guidance, and each evening she says the same prayer, asking her angel to guard her each night. Marie believes that her life has been a series of gentle and timely interventions from her angel, and she feels truly guided through life.

When Marie was a teenager during the Second World War, she worked picking potatoes in her native Yorkshire. At the age of sixteen, she formed a close friendship with Joseph, an Italian prisoner of war who was also working on the land. Their friendship blossomed into a significant relationship but sadly it faded when Joseph was repatriated after the war. Still, life went on for Marie; time passed and she planned to train as a teacher.

Synchronicity now comes into play in Marie's story, as one day she was invited to travel with her Uncle Tom to meet a relative who lived some distance away. To her surprise who should also be on the bus but her Italian friend Joseph! They quickly fell into conversation and it finally emerged that he had written to Marie when he had returned to England, as he had hoped to renew their friendship, but, fearing that his return would ruin her daughter's plans to train as a teacher, Marie's mother had hidden his letter to her. Had Marie not caught the bus that day, she would never have known of Joseph's return.

Their meeting in such an unlikely way seemed like a friendly nudge from Marie's guardian angel, propelling her in the right direction. By the age of twenty-two, she had married Joseph, which was the beginning of a long and wonderfully happy union. 'Uncle Tom was the unlikely earth angel,' she jokes, as it was the trip with him that led to this lovely partnership.

Their marriage was so happy that when Joseph died some thirty-five years later Marie was inconsolable, totally devastated by her loss. Over the years she and Joseph had travelled many times to visit his beloved Italy and his family there, and Marie had come to love that beautiful country. Therefore, she decided after Joseph's death to travel to Italy once more with their daughter. It was a bitter-sweet experience and Marie had conflicting emotions as to how she would be affected by returning to the village where Joseph had been born and his family still lived.

It was the feast day of San Rocco when Marie arrived in the village, and everyone went to the village church. It was when Marie walked down the aisle to receive communion that the most amazing thing happened. She was completely overwhelmed by the sense of her husband's presence. So strong was this sensation that she automatically turned around, expecting to see him! Sensations of total peace and joy filled her heart; all her sadness and anxiety evaporated in the wonderful atmosphere.

For the rest of Marie's stay in that little village, she felt only sensations of tranquillity and happiness, as she had on previous visits with her husband. Marie believes an angel was sent by Joseph that day to comfort her in her grief. She has been eternally grateful for the experience ever since.

Shine On, Star of Gratitude

If we can find a glimmer of gratitude in our hearts, even the most trying of situations can become a touch more bearable. Gratitude makes us realise that we are not necessarily at the mercy of our surroundings; that there is much for us to be thankful for in our lives, whatever our circumstances. Gratitude can help us to move from a victim mentality to one of empowerment, in which we know that we too are at the receiving end of the Universe's goodness. We are truly blessed.

STAR POINTS TO PONDER:

I give thanks for another day.

I count my blessings on a daily basis.

I treat others with kindness and gratitude.

I am developing all and any gifts that I have been granted.

I tell my loved ones how much I appreciate them.

I say thank you to the many unsung heroes I meet each day.

I will smile at a stranger and ask them to pass it on!

4

The Star of Trust

Trust is the essence of Win–Win relationships

because you trust others and they trust you,

you can be open, you can put your cards on the table.

Even though you may see things differently,

you're committed to understanding each other's viewpoints.

Stephen R. Covey
Author

Learning to Trust

Our fourth star is all about trust, which is not always an easy option. We may have had bitter experiences in the past that make it difficult for us to trust anyone or anything. Close relationships involve issues of trust and if we feel we have been let down, it can often be an enormous problem to begin to trust again. And if we have difficulty in trusting those who we can see around us, how much harder will it be to put our trust in ethereal angels?

Trust may sometimes mean placing our faith in intangibles and unknown quantities. If we are prey to debilitating feelings of fear that root us to our current position, it can be particularly hard to trust others. Trust is often about letting go of control and standing back, which can be difficult to do when we are troubled by doubts and uncertainties. However, we can begin by learning to have confidence in what we do know – ourselves. Learning to trust ourselves is the first step, as having faith in our own judgements will afford us greater freedom to trust the judgement of others. We start living when we start believing.

Once we have learned to trust ourselves, we can begin to ask for help in the knowledge that we really do not have to go it alone; the Universe is on our side. With practice, it will become easier to recognise the help that comes to us in the guise of heavenly signs from a Higher Source. As we grow more confident in the strength of our intuitive powers and our connection with the angelic realms, we will soon realise that we naturally have the ability and knowledge to act upon these signs from above.

There are steps in this chapter to take you along the path towards trust. If you are discerning, ready to trust your instincts and ask the angels for help, clarity will be yours.

Allow and empower someone you trust

to guide you on your path.

Cherie Carter-Scott PhD
Life coach and motivational speaker

> ## Divine Star
>
> In each moment, no matter what our circumstances are, we have the choice to live in trust or live in fear. Trust is rooted in confidence – knowing that we are doing everything in our power, and letting go. Fear is rooted in doubt.

Letting Go of Fear and Living with Trust

Fear shows up hand-in-hand with worry and anxiety. Whether a circumstance is beyond your control, or you are still doing what you can to shape a situation, in a way you are continually standing at a fork in the road where you're faced with two options: the path of fear or the path of trust. The path you choose will help you create your reality.

How does this work? The Universe is a reflector. It shows us the energy we project. If you choose to live in trust, the vision you're trusting and putting energy into is what the Universe will mirror back to you.

To trust in life itself is to choose a path of love, a path of curiosity and wonder. When you live in trust, you open yourself up to the magic of the Universe. To trust life is to come to the point of letting go.

It's about BELIEVING and RECEIVING.

When you live in trust, you detach yourself from the details. You stop worrying, and you stop being concerned with the question of 'how'. You live confidently, open to the magic of this life. In order to trust life, you will also have to let go of any inclination to make assumptions, particularly assumptions that assign value to your experiences. If you find yourself constantly categorising experiences as 'good' or 'bad' you may want to consider how much, at the very core of yourself, you trust the process of life.

Without a doubt, every one of us goes through periods in our life that are difficult. We face circumstances that bring us to our knees, and we find ourselves in situations that could easily make us question the fairness of life. Yet we have a choice. We can get caught up in judging all of our experiences and circumstances, in assigning value to every situation we're in, or we can decide to see things from a more objective and trusting perspective.

Each situation is what it is . . . that's all! It doesn't have to be good or bad, it can just be. Each circumstance you're in right now simply is what it is. Rather than spending energy assigning value to it and maintaining assumptions, you can choose to move through the experience, simply by experiencing it and living it.

As you let go of any need to assign value to your experiences and begin to observe how life truly works, you will find yourself beginning to trust in life. You may even start to believe that everything does happen for a reason, that there is divine order in events. You may find yourself in the space of trusting that everything, in the end, works out for the best. That all of your experiences are leading you to more knowledge, wisdom, love, harmony, peace, gratitude, courage and trust. Along the way, the more you affirm these realities in every cell of your body and with every core belief you have, the more you will witness them.

Imagine the doors that open and the magic that comes into your life when you trust in life and how it works. The more you trust, the more you will have reason to trust. What may begin as a leap of faith will soon be grounded in reality with tangible proof. That's how the Universe works. It reflects the energy you project; it reflects your belief system back to you.

While there is much that is beyond our control, the one thing we can always control is how we choose to perceive life and all of our experiences. Rather than draining your energy assigning value to each step on your path, consider spending the energy living each step of the way, feeling and experiencing. When we replace the need to live in fear and worry with confidence and trust in life, we create the space necessary to witness and appreciate the miracles happening in every moment of our lives.

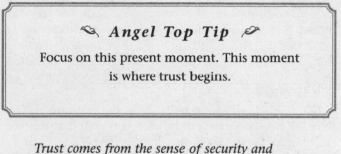

❧ *Angel Top Tip* ❧

Focus on this present moment. This moment
is where trust begins.

Trust comes from the sense of security and safety we receive from others. Trust can free us to move when fear overwhelms our desire to participate in the exciting challenges of life.

Kathleen Keating
Therapist and author

Angels of Trust and Synchronicity

Glennyce recently had an experience that demonstrates how, when we stop judging our circumstances and simply go with the flow of them, our trust in the Universe may be amply rewarded:

I had been invited to give a talk for a bookshop in Crewe, Cheshire, and had worked out exactly which train would take me from Manchester to arrive in good time for the talk. Having carefully checked on the platform monitor that this was the train I needed, I settled down in my seat and glanced around, realising that the train would soon be very full indeed. At this point a rail employee entered the carriage to tell us that the train would not be going to Crewe after all and that we all had to alight. Amidst a lot of groaning, my fellow passengers and I got off and watched as the train rattled off into the distance completely empty.

But another train soon pulled in at the platform and we were informed over the public address system that this was the train for Crewe. Everyone climbed aboard and began to settle again, only to be told minutes later that we would have to alight once more, because this train was going to York.

The grumbling was considerably louder this time, especially as there was now no new train in sight. Glancing at my watch, I felt my heart sink; all this time-wasting would surely make me late for the talk. My palms began to sweat and I felt a slight nervous panic set in. Just then, music was switched on over the public address system: it was Abba singing 'I believe in Angels'. I smiled to myself and said silently, 'OK, I trust you to sort this out for me.' At that precise moment a train came into view and for the third time we all climbed aboard and found our seats.

Off we went and the guard announced that, owing to the problems experienced, this would be an express train travelling directly to Crewe. I arrived at Crewe with time to spare and the good friend who I feared would be waiting and worrying for me at the station had in fact only just arrived. I certainly didn't fail to thank the angels for rewarding my trust in them!

Divine Star

Trust is an experience that occurs when we enter a present moment of awareness, and are able to perceive the energetic experience and connection between cause and effect. The power of trust is always present.

Heavenly Signs

It is never easy to trust. This applies not only to our circumstances and those around us, but also to ourselves. Trusting ourselves is often the hardest thing of all. We may lack confidence in our judgements, and fail to follow our inner voice or instincts, in which case the problem grows.

However, we are given signs from a Higher Source all the time; it is just a matter of recognising them and going with the flow. As angels are present in all our lives we simply have to trust that their messages will be revealed to us when we submit to the concept.

Sometimes angelic signs can be so subtle that it is tempting to dismiss them out of hand. Yet if we listen to our instincts and trust ourselves to tune into these signs, and then believe them when we receive them, they will increase in frequency and it will become easier to understand them.

Signs can come to us in the form of music, such as a piece of music that has particular associations for us and which we hear unexpectedly on the radio or television. Many people have told us that when a sad event occurs such as the breakdown of a relationship or the loss of a loved one, they have heard their 'special song'. Some of these people have said that initially they thought hearing the song was just a strange coincidence, but when they decided to trust that it was in fact a message, they found that they heard it more and more at precisely those times when they most needed comfort.

Your own special sign may be music or take the form of an aspect of nature, such as a certain type of butterfly, a rainbow, flower or bird. It could even be a number that frequently appears in your life, smelling a special perfume that has no obvious source, or, perhaps the most obvious one of all, a feather.

Feathers appear to be the most frequent of all types of angelic communication; they are gentle symbols which are unlikely to cause fear and yet speak to us dramatically. The white feather features in so many angel stories that it has been labelled 'the angels' calling card'. It is visually a very powerful sign that often appears in the most unlikely places and cannot fail to be recognised. There are remarkable accounts of feathers lying on the grass in the pouring rain and yet being quite dry when picked up. They also appear inexplicably inside handbags, drawers and cupboards that have not been opened for some time and even inside shoes. These are all mysterious signs, yet soothing and reaffirming that we are never alone if we simply trust.

If you ask for a sign that the angels are with you it will frequently appear in the form of a feather. Trust this sign and it will occur again whenever you need it most. Receive these and all other angelic signs for what they are, messages from a spiritual source, and they will appear again and again for you.

So do not be afraid to ask for help: the angels are ever waiting for you to approach them and they will be swift to reply. You really have nothing to fear if you let go and trust the angels. Life can feel so full of joy and fulfilment when we release our deepest fears and trust the angels to guide us. We only have to ask.

AFFIRMATION

Today, I have trust that everything is planned in a way that supports my Highest Good. I am secure in knowing that the world is a safe and wonderful place.

EXERCISE:
Ask for a Sign

* Start your personal journey of trust by asking for a sign. When it appears write about it in your Angel Journal. Note down what exactly you asked for, what happened, when it happened, your mood at the time and how your feelings were affected by the experience. Do this each time the sign appears.

* After a few weeks, read through your journal entries. You may see a pattern emerging, consolidating your belief and trust. The older you are, the more obvious the pattern may be. You may find the pattern has been present in your life for many years; you just subconsciously chose to ignore it. There might even be a clue as far back as childhood, linking into your life today and assuring you that the pattern is in place.

Be a guiding star above me,

Illuminate each rock and tide,

Guide my ship across the waters

To the waveless harbourside.

Caitlin Matthews
Author and Celtic authority

The Stairway to Heaven?

Here is a story to illustrate how obvious angelic signs and patterns can be, once we know how to recognise them for what they are.

The sign for Pam could not have been clearer and the emerging pattern leaves her in little doubt that the angels are very close to her indeed. Early in 2006 Pam and her husband Roy decided to move from their home in England and settle on the beautiful island of Tenerife. This had been a long-held ambition and, like so many people, when retirement enabled the move they took the opportunity and realised their dream.

The move happened in a whirl and they had only just settled into their apartment when they received news from relatives in Canada, who explained that they would love to come and stay with them, hopefully arriving shortly. It was with mixed emotions that Pam agreed to the visit. These were to be their very first guests and although she loved them dearly, she was very worried that she wouldn't be an especially good hostess at such a confusing time. It would be fun, however, and Pam started to plan what they would do, and where they would eat.

Pam and Roy had discovered their own favourite restaurant on the island, in an idyllic location, overlooking the entire valley of Orotava. The building was part of a sixteenth-century monastery called El Monasteerio, and this appeared to be the perfect place to start a holiday with their guests.

In the event, it was lovely to welcome their relatives to their new home and, as planned, Pam and Roy took them to the very special restaurant for dinner on the first evening. Not normally a nervous person in the slightest, Pam nevertheless felt extremely unsettled as they sat at their table. Excusing herself for a moment, she went to the ladies' room below stairs for a moment to catch her breath. A quiet moment or two would help to compose her and she said a little prayer, asking for help to make this a special and happy holiday for her relatives.

Making her way back upstairs, Pam turned a corner and, to her amazement, there in the very centre of the step next to the top one – virtually at Pam's eye level – was a beautiful, curly, fluffy white feather. Her heart lifted and she picked up the feather, certain that this was the sign she needed to tell her all would be well. Indeed the holiday was wonderful and enjoyed by everyone.

Some time later, old friends from England also came to stay for a holiday. This time Pam felt settled and confident that she would be a perfect hostess. Once more they took their visitors to this special place to eat. After a delicious meal, Pam once more went to visit the ladies' room. She remembered when she had found her feather after asking for help. This time, however, it occurred to her that she had no need to ask. Climbing the stairs to the dining room again, Pam was sure her angel would never be far away. Turning the corner of the staircase, again she was stopped in her tracks by the sight of a beautiful, fluffy, pure white feather. It lay right in the middle of the very same step as before! Picking up the feather, Pam says she cradled it in her palm in what can only be described as a daze. The sign was so very clear and heart-warming. The amazing fact is, Pam says, that the stairs are highly polished, with an open tread, and the slightest breeze or movement would have wafted a delicate feather away in a trice.

As if the two feathers were not enough to convince Pam that her angel was watching over her and sending her messages, it happened for the third time. This time was slightly different from the previous occasions but equally significant. A very old friend with whom they had lost touch for many years appeared out of the blue, as it were, and once more Pam and Roy took their guest to the restaurant for dinner. Visiting the ladies' as usual, Pam climbed the stairs and, sure enough, there on the very same step, in the very same position, right in the middle, was a feather. However, this time the feather was a beautiful brown colour. Picking it up, Pam placed it in her pocket and decided that when she returned home she would take a look in our book *An Angel Forever*, which she knew included a list explaining the significance of feather colours. Smiling as she opened the book that evening, she read that brown is a symbol of healing, which was appropriate as their friendship with their guest had been healed after many years apart.

There have been other feathers in Pam's life, which seems to emphasise the fact that if we recognise an angelic sign for what it is, and indeed ask for a sign, they will appear in our lives with more frequency. There may already have been signs in your own life that you may have fleetingly suspected to have contained messages for you, but which you nevertheless ignored at the time. Trust your angel, ask for a sign, believe you will be heard and for certain you will find your answer through a sign and pattern that is right for you.

Seekers are offered clues all the time from the world of the spirits.

Ordinary people call these clues coincidences.

Deepak Chopra M.D.
Doctor and spiritual teacher

✎ *Angel Top Tip* ✐

Next time you are in the garden or walking in
the countryside, look for your very own white
feather. Place it in a spot where you will see it
daily. It will encourage the angels to visit.
Expect miracles in your life. When a small one
appears, say thank you and be prepared for
bigger ones to follow.

Are You Looking Deeply Enough?

There is a spiritual pattern in all of our lives which may be
likened to the DNA of our soul. However, this pattern may be
of a very subtle nature and if we do not look consciously for it
we may never uncover it. Moreover, as we leave childhood
behind we often become more likely to ignore or dismiss our
intuitive feelings. Our sense of magic or mystery may become
diminished, and our awareness of the spiritual increasingly
hidden from view by the clutter of daily life. The good news is
that it is never too late to find your own particular spiritual
pattern.

Allow the angels to give you a gentle nudge by thinking

back. There may be a single moment in your childhood that stands out. Perhaps you have always felt drawn to a particular activity, person or emotional event that holds a fascination for you. Take a close look at the past; could there even be a musical clue such as a refrain running through your life unrecognised? Have you a talent but your lack of confidence has held you back from displaying it to a wider audience? Does a certain person drift in and out of your life at intervals when you least expect to see them? May they hold the clue: look a little deeper into their unexpected appearances. On the other hand, your particular sign could be located in nature or at a specific geographical location, such as somewhere you feel comfortable and drawn towards. Ponder this in quiet moments.

We know two friends of some thirty years' acquaintance who keep in touch only spasmodically. However, they know their spiritual patterns are intertwined and that sooner or later their paths will cross again. Their relationship is symbiotic and even through times when they have lived many miles apart, sooner or later they have received a signal or sign that they need to work together again. They tell us that they feel no need to keep a close form of contact, conscious as they are that angels will move them together when the time is right – rather like chess pieces.

The friends represent an amazing manifestation of trust and that indeed is the key to finding the pattern. Continue to write down any little incident or sign that you could conceive as a clue in your Angel Journal. It may take a little time but the pattern will emerge. Most importantly, you must truly believe that all will be revealed to you. Have faith: the angels are there to help. You only have to ask them. In short, it's all a matter of trust.

MEDITATION:
A Walk in the Gardens of Trust

This meditation is designed to help you trust that your life is unfolding as it should, that there is a connection between all the events in your life.

* As you close your eyes, take a long . . . deep . . . breath . . . Feel your body relaxing as you continue to breathe slowly and deeply. Breathing in . . . and breathing out . . . Release any tension; allow passing thoughts to drift away.

* Feel the golden energy of the Earth coming up through the soles of your feet, moving up through your entire body. Feel how this golden energy grounds you, creating a space of safety, creating a connection to all that is.

* Now feel energetic light from the loving source of the Universe coming down through the top of your head, filling your entire body. See the colour of this light, and know this is the perfect colour for you at this moment. Feel how this light energy fills you with love.

* See yourself in a wide, open space, filled with beauty. In this space of peace and stillness, bring into your awareness a circumstance in your life that you resent. Take a deep breath and ask for the conscious awareness of which assumptions you have been making about the circumstance. Have you assigned the circumstance as 'bad' or 'not fair'? Be aware of which words or phrases appear before you. As you recognise the words before you, feel the emotional charge that connects them to you. Notice the heaviness of the emotional charge . . .

* When you are ready, affirm that you no longer desire to make assumptions or spend energy assigning value to each experience. Feel the heaviness lifting and watch

the words in front of you fade into nothingness. Feel the chaos dissolving, opening up space for clarity and peace within you.

* In the newly created space within you, take a moment now to step back and gently observe the situation in your life from a distance. Allow yourself to view the situation from an objective perspective. Feel your body filling with gratitude and love. Feel the perfection of this moment.

* As you move out of this meditation, talk a long, deep breath. Affirm your trust in life and the workings of the Universe. Know that the Universe, through the miracles it manifests, has begun to reflect this trusting vision back to you. Miracles are taking place right now in this very moment. The miracles will continue to manifest as you continue to live in trust.

Discover the blessings you already have.

Cherie Carter-Scott PhD
Life coach and motivational speaker

Divine Star

Maybe all that we really need to do to bring
the angels a little nearer to us is to create some
personal space, both physically and mentally.
We may need to clear the decks and give
ourselves time to breathe spiritually. Everyone
deserves a little time to themselves, no matter
how busy their lives are. If we are determined
to find time this can be achieved.

Begin by finding just ten minutes at some
point in the day to sit in quiet contemplation
and ask your angel to be with you. If you
manage to do this on a regular basis, not only
will you feel a little calmer each day but also
the signs and symbols of your angels will
become more obvious to you.

A Bird of Paradise

Like Pam in our last story, Gemma is another person who
became aware of a pattern of connections unfolding in her
life.

Gemma was fortunate enough to grow up in the beautiful
English Lake District. As a little child she was always
surrounded by fauna and flora. She loved the birds that visited
her garden and would remember the names of birds pointed
out to her by her parents and older siblings when she walked
along the lakeside close to her home. Her particular favourite

was the tiny, brilliant blue kingfisher, the sight of which never failed to excite her.

Eventually, Gemma left her beautiful home for university and then found a job in London. However, there always appeared to be a kingfisher connection in her life. For her birthday, she would often receive small ornaments of them or cards decorated with lovely bird illustrations.

The pattern was not, however, uppermost in Gemma's mind when she found herself getting ready for her wedding at the age of twenty-five. The wedding was to take place in London, for not only did her husband's family live there, but by that time Gemma's family had also moved to the capital.

Gemma's big day dawned with sunshine and blue skies; it was a perfect spring morning and she got dressed in great excitement. More or less everything was in place, and she had only to await the arrival of her flowers from the local florist, when all would be ready. At last the doorbell rang and the beaming florist handed the flowers to Gemma's mother. Carefully she placed the boxes containing the bouquets for the bridesmaids, the buttonholes for the family and the beautiful bridal posy on the kitchen table.

Lifting her own flowers from the box, Gemma gave a little gasp of pleasure and recognition, for there, nestling amongst the flowers, was a tiny blue toy kingfisher. It was then she noticed for the first time that the name of the florist's shop was actually 'Kingfishers'! The day was made completely perfect, she believed, by the discovery that the angels had revealed themselves through her beloved little bird.

AFFIRMATION

Today, I have trust that everything is planned in a way that supports my highest good. I am secure in knowing that the world is a safe and wonderful place.

Communication with angels starts

if you recognise they are there.

Murray Steinman
Writer

Colour and Angels

In both Gemma and Pam's stories of angelic encounters, colour plays a role. For Gemma it was the magnificent blue of her kingfisher connection; for Pam the brown and white of the feathers she found. As we have seen, different colours often carry different associations in angelic encounters.

The connection between colour and angels has a long tradition. The theologian and mystic Emanuel Swedenborg taught that the colours of the garments of angels correspond to their intelligence. These colours range from pastels and white through to flame and gold.

Here are the colours attributed to the seven archangels:

Michael	Blue
Jophiel	Yellow
Chamuuel	Pink
Gabriel	White

Raphael	Green
Uriel	Purple and Gold
Zadkiel	Violet

Others claim the colours of the angels' garments correspond to their position in the heavenly hierarchy.

Besides their magnificent robes and the wings that prove them to be more than human, angels in religious art are often depicted with halos. It is believed by some that the halos are really depictions of auras. An aura is the 'atmosphere' or subtle energy that surrounds each living being. Some people today claim to have the ability to see human auras and others go so far as to say that this ability can be taught to others. According to those who work with auras, the colours and their intensity reflect the physical and emotional state of a person. The first layer of the aura is red, relating to the physical body and sexuality. Orange is the second layer, representing the life force or metabolic body. Yellow represents the emotional energies and the soul of the individual. Green is the colour of balance and connects the ego to the Higher Self. Turquoise represents the inspirational self, blue represents motivation and violet represents the true essence or Higher Consciousness.

The aura is often linked to the chakras, the invisible circles of energy in the body that are believed to absorb and transform the universal energy known as *prana* or chi. The oriental word 'chakra' means wheel or disc and the chakras are still referred to in many meditative practices such as yoga. The main chakras number seven in total and are represented by seven colours of light. Yoga teaches that the seven chakras are as follows:

Base chakra	red
Sacral chakra	orange
Solar plexus chakra	yellow
Heart chakra	green or pink

Throat chakra	turquoise
Brow chakra	blue
Crown chakra	violet

The crown or top of the head is clearly the nearest part of the body to the spiritual world and, interestingly, many angelic experiences include descriptions of angels in blue or purple gowns.

AFFIRMATION

Today, I trust my choices are guided by angelic inspiration, and I experience success.

The Ethereal Light

Many people report angelic experiences that contain lights of different colours. The light may appear as an individual colour, as an array of colours or as a vision of pure white.

From early childhood, Dulce has seen unusual lights. She describes seeing beautiful twinkling white lights in trees when she was a little girl, which clearly had a great effect on her. Although life has not always been kind to Dulce, the unexpected appearance of the lights has always felt gentle and reassuring. Recently, however, Dulce saw a most unusual light whilst involved in Reiki healing. She describes this light as a 'beautiful dusky pink' that was translucent and appeared in the shape of a butterfly. As you can imagine, it was a profoundly moving experience.

Sometime later, on a hot summer's day, Dulce was in her bedroom, trying to find a place in the house where she could cool off. To her amazement, suddenly a light appeared in mid air. It was similar to the pink one she had seen earlier, but this time it was a wonderful shade of blue. Again, the light was translucent and the shape reminiscent of a butterfly. It was, says Dulce, an absolutely unforgettable experience. She felt such a sense of wonder at this vision of remarkable beauty.

Blue is regarded as a highly spiritual colour and pink represents love, so these incidents represent very close encounters with the angels indeed. Talking to Dulce about these experiences, Gary and I have hopefully convinced her that the angels in shapes of coloured light were very close to her. 'Do you really think so?' said Dulce.

'Trust me!' I said.

Their garments are white, but with an unearthly whiteness. I cannot describe it because it cannot be compared to earthly whiteness; it is much softer to the eye. These bright angels are enveloped in a light so different to ours that by comparison everything else seems dark. When you see a band of fifty, you are lost in amazement. They seem clothed with golden plates constantly moving like so many suns.

Père Lamy
Parish priest (d.1931)

Switching on the Light

In angelic encounters the appearance of light often gives rise to confusion, even though it most commonly appears when the recipient is in a spiritual state or employed in a spiritual occupation. Reiki practitioners, for instance, frequently describe seeing lights and feeling a spiritual presence in the room, as Dulce did in her encounter. Light perceived in such situations is most often described as an intense bright, white light. Less frequently, the light is of a gentle colour.

Light is the very essence of the angels and has always been a source of wonder. Both starlight and sunlight have played central roles in the history of human progress. Astonishingly, it has been revealed that the Vikings may have used special crystals called sunstones to navigate by in cloudy weather. By holding a crystal up to the sun and rotating it, researchers replicating this theory found that a viewer would be able to track the sun all day long. Even if the sky is full of clouds or moisture, the polarisation of the sunlight changes very little.

We now know that the Universe is filled with energy in the form of electromagnetic waves of light. These waves of light are not visible to the human eye, but we know for certain that they are there. Isaac Newton famously discovered that directing sunlight through a prism reveals that white light can be split into the seven colours of the rainbow, with each colour vibrating at a different frequency.

If the electromagnetic waves at each end of the spectrum are invisible to the human eye and yet we can feel the effects of their presence, why should this not apply to angels? They are after all beings of pure light and energy. It seems reasonable to assume that although invisible to the naked eye, like electromagnetic waves, they are similarly around us at all times. Do these magical beings simply alter their frequency when allowing us to see them?

In Yellowknife, Canada, something remarkable has been documented. It involves the wonderful light display of the aurora borealis, known as the 'Northern Lights'. The Northern Lights take the form of waves of colour in the sky, unparalleled in nature. They originate as the earth's atmosphere is buffeted by energetic particles from magnetic storms in space. Research in Yellowknife found that a large percentage of people living in the area could not only see the aurora borealis, but 'hear' it also! These people were amazed to discover that not everyone could actually hear the wonderful lights in the way that they could. What they heard was incredibly beautiful music, unlike anything they heard from any other source. Several people commented that they believed this to be the sound of angels singing!

Scientists are still trying to unravel many of the mysteries associated with the aurora borealis and space physics. In an attempt to understand this phenomenon further, several spacecraft have been launched. Wouldn't it be marvellous if those on board reported hearing singing whilst they are in orbit!

The lights and colours often associated with angels suggest that they may be able to divide at will the radiant white light that is associated with them into a variety of shades. Maybe one day science will even invent a machine to detect angelic presence.

The angels are the dispensers and administrators of the divine beneficence towards us; they regard our safety, undertake our defence, direct our ways, and exercise a constant solicitude that no evil befalls us.

John Calvin
Theologian (1509–1564)

EXERCISE:
Sip Angel Sunshine

You can literally drink in colour in the form of Angel
Sunshine Water. To do this, you will need:

Distilled water or purified tap water

A clean, clear glass bottle and sheets of transparent,
coloured plastic – e.g. red, orange, yellow, green, blue,
indigo, purple (obtainable from art shops)

Or clean, coloured glass bottles

A marker pen (optional)

Sunshine

To create your own drink of angel sunshine, wrap a sheet of
the coloured plastic around a glass bottle or find a coloured
bottle that suits your purposes. Choose a colour that you
intuitively feel links with the angel whose qualities you
want to bring into your life, such as red perhaps for the
Angel of Courage or blue for the Angel of Trust. If you wish,
you can write the angel's name onto the plastic sheet or
bottle with a marker pen. Alternatively, you can look up the
list of colours associated with the archangels under the section 'Colour and Angels' on page 121 or simply work your
way through the colours of the rainbow.

∗ Fill the bottle with the distilled water. Put a stopper on it
and leave it in the sunshine for a couple of hours, so that
the rays of sun warm the water through. (Check to make
sure that the bottle won't act as a magnifying glass and
inadvertently start a fire!)

∗ Whenever you want to bring the qualities of your chosen
angel to mind, take a few sips of your Angel Sunshine
Water, trusting your angels to bring you the strength you
need.

Asking is the beginning of receiving.

Through a simple believing prayer, you can change your future.

Dr Bruce Wilkinson
Theologian and author

Building a Bridge to Heaven

Even with the support of the angels it may take time for you to build up trust. Be patient: if you have spent most of your life in doubt then solid unequivocal trust will not be yours overnight. Remember that the most important thing is not what happens to you in life, but how you deal with and respond to what happens. One small step at a time may be the best way forward. Be determined; there is nothing that you cannot change if you really wish to. No situation can hold you back if you truly believe and trust that spiritual help is at hand.

Your thoughts are your own – no one else can control them. Thought initiates action, so the more positive your thoughts, the more positive your actions. If you show others signs of trust, they in turn will begin to trust you. This generates a circle of trustworthiness, which will lead to a better understanding of those close to you. So start today by taking a small step towards trust in others, in the Universe and particularly in your angel. The exercise below will help you to change your mindset from one of distrust and lack to trust and abundance.

Think big, there are unseen forces ready to
support your dreams.

Cheryl Richardson
Personal coach, lecturer and author

EXERCISE:
Trusting in the Natural Abundance of Life

Prosperity, trust and abundance are our natural state, although it may not always seem like it! When others place demands on us, when the bills pile up on the doorstep and money is tight, it can be hard to trust in the support, guidance and goodness of the Universe.

Do you sometimes feel that life has been unfair or is moving too fast for you? Do you find yourself not having enough time or money? Here are some easy steps to encourage trust and abundance to flow readily into your life once more.

1. *Do prosperity and trust seem like a myth to you?* Do you believe that prosperity and abundance belong in fairy tales or to a chosen few (but not you!) in real life?

   Solution: Listen carefully to your Inner Angel – you have the power to create your personal riches in life through your thoughts and attitude, and to create your own happy ending.

2. *Do you believe that this world is a place of scarcity and lack?* Does it seem harsh and unfair?

   Solution: Prosperity is about more than just money or material things, about the 'haves' and 'have nots'. The world is a very rich and beautiful place – just look around you. Think about the beauty of the sky, the greenery all around you and the grace of the animal kingdom, all of which are priceless. Trust that you belong to the natural order of things, and you are part of the abundance and harmony of the Universe.

3. *Do you feel permanently dissatisfied?* Do you find it difficult to trust that you could ever feel otherwise?

Solution: When did you last feel a sense of wellbeing and satisfaction? Ask yourself what brought about those feelings of contentment. Imagine feeling like that now – satisfied and content. Stay with your feelings. When you are feeling prosperous you will be positive, generous and upbeat, radiating feelings of trust, open-heartedness and abundance, thereby bringing more good things into your life.

4. *Is prosperity out of reach for you?* Do you believe that you are destined to go without?

Solution: How would you feel if your life was magnificent, abundant, fulfilled and spiritually sound? Would it be too much, too little or, maybe just right for you? Don't wait for something or someone else to give you permission to have it all. To create oneness or flow in your life, your mind, body and belief system must work in harmony, in utter trust that abundance and prosperity are truly your natural inheritance.

5. *Do you lurch from one financial crisis to another?* Do you feel that you will always suffer from limited resources?

Solution: Every time a financial crisis arises, shift your attention to a potentially positive resolution or existing blessing in your life. Give something away with no concern about lack, and perform a random act of kindness for someone. Your kind actions will attract similar kindnesses to come your way and will also prove to you that you always have plenty of resources, whether or not you have money in the bank.

6. *Are feelings of low self-worth affecting your ability to trust in the goodness of life?* Do you feel undeserving of the rewards that life has to offer?

Solution: When we feel unworthy we create a void of self-belief. However, every spiritual being has many riches flowing through them at every moment. You too are a spiritual being, with riches flowing through you at this moment. Use your mind, that powerful instrument, to discover what these riches are. What is it that brings you a sense of personal satisfaction? Can you identify those feelings?

7. *Do you sometimes feel very alone?* Do you wish you had the support and encouragement of others?

Solution: You may feel as though you are having to cope alone. Begin by asking your angels for help when a difficult or stressful situation arises, then relax and trust your angels to take control. Look for signs of an angelic presence in your life. You may be by yourself, but you are not alone.

AFFIRMATION

I deserve to get one hundred per cent out of everything I do.

I deserve to have an incredible life!

Learning to Let Go: Anne's Feather

There are times when it can nevertheless be very difficult to trust that life is fair, or that we live in a generous and supportive Universe. The loss of a loved one in particular can stir up many emotions and issues relating to trust.

Each individual experiences mourning differently. Some people may withdraw from family and friends in order to be alone in their grief. Others may wish to talk incessantly about the loved one they have lost. The time needed to recover from a bereavement also varies dramatically from person to person, although we all simply have to trust that one day our loss will hurt less and our memories will become easier to bear and less painful:

Anne had struggled to come to terms with the death of her much-loved father, Robert. His illness had been distressing but the vacuum he left in Anne's heart was huge. One way of coping with the distress was to visit her sister daily, knowing that she understood exactly how Anne was feeling. Months passed and the sadness and feeling of 'nerves' were with her still.

One day her sister suggested they go for a walk and Anne readily agreed, as fresh air and nature always helped to soothe her. The women ventured deep into the countryside and at one point came across a very large, beautiful tree. Drawn to it, Anne was thrilled to discover a huge, white feather lying at its base. Picking this up, she placed it in her handbag and took it home. She vowed to keep it, confident that it was a sign from the angels.

Some five years later Anne's life was in turmoil and she found that her 'nerves' were getting the better of her again. However, she was about to embark on a holiday in the Lake District, which she hoped would calm her. After packing her case and cleaning the entire house, she was ready to leave. Imagine her astonishment when she noticed a very large white feather lying on her kitchen mat in the exact spot that she had carefully vacuumed only moments before! Picking up the feather, she felt calm sweep over her. She knew that once again the angels were there when she needed them most.

Arriving at her holiday destination, she unpacked her case in the company of her sister. She told her the story of the feather, adding how fortunate she felt that the sign was once more so obvious. At that very moment, she lifted her makeup bag and there, sitting beneath it, she found yet another lovely white feather.

Trusting the angels has become an important part of Anne's life.

EXERCISE:
Write Your Own Commitment to Trust

Trust begins with you. In your Angel Journal or below, write a short encouraging note to yourself, stating how proud you are of yourself for making a commitment to the work in this book, and how much you appreciate your courage and willingness to grow and experience your own greatness.

'MY COMMITMENT TO TRUST' STATEMENT

_____

_____

_____

_____

_____

My signature   Date

Going Forwards in Trust

To let trust into your life, begin by slowing down and letting go a little. You don't have to control everything in your life with a rod of iron. This doesn't mean that you should shirk your responsibilities; just take a step back now and then to allow events to unfold around you without forcing them. Allow the voices of others to be heard; you may be surprised at what you learn when you start to listen. And open your eyes: the Universe is forever sending you messages through the subtle signs and symbols that surround you.

Above all, trust that the angels are by your side right now, simply waiting for you to welcome them into your life.

STAR POINTS TO PONDER:

I trust the angels to guide me through each day.

I trust my own judgement.

I have faith in the kindness of others.

I ask my friends for advice and trust their judgement.

I have confidence in my dream and will follow it.

I will learn to delegate and trust that the work will be done.

I live in a prosperous and abundant world.

❧ 5 ❧

The Star of Courage

To be successful in your chosen career or work endeavour, you must release any present Karmic conditioning that declares 'I can't do this'.
You can!

Deepak Chopra M.D.
Doctor and spiritual teacher

Learning to Be Courageous

*T*he Star of Courage concerns a quality that comes in many shapes and guises, from the everyday, such as braving a trip to the dentist, to coping with life-changing events such as financial crisis and loss. One thing is for sure: there will be testing times in all of our lives when courage will be required of us.

At these challenging moments we may be tempted to look towards the courageous deeds of men and women throughout history for inspiration. But whilst we may look outside ourselves for guidance, we can all be sure that we possess unplumbed and hidden depths of courage within ourselves.

However, it may require a little effort to realise our inner potential.

Fortunately, there are various steps we can take to help us become more attuned to our inner resources of bravery and fortitude.

Acknowledge that you are the source of your manifestations.

Cherie Carter-Scott PhD
Life coach and motivational speaker

✎ *Angel Top Tip* ✎

There is a kind of natural courage that comes from facing our mistakes and the mistakes of others with honesty and serenity. When we recognise this we will be less disturbed by the actions or words of others. It will give us the courage to turn within so that we may release the past and trust the now.

Everyday Courage

Even if we never fully comprehend the full extent to which we each affect the world, it is a mistake to think that our everyday lives don't matter or have no effect on others. We must start to think as powerful beings, because that's truly who we are. You too are nothing less that an extraordinary, powerful being.

What do you desire? Who do you desire to be?

Clarity is power. Once you know what you desire, the path will be simple. Move out of 'the middle'. If the beginning lies in knowing what you desire, the middle stage relates to all the questions you raise in wondering how you'll achieve what you desire. The middle stage is that of worry, the stage of fear: 'How can I possibly make this happen? What if it doesn't work?' The mind can come up with many obstacles and excuses.

Now is the time to forget all the 'maybes' and 'some days' and 'I don't knows'. Move out of the middle. It's a mindset. That is all. Begin with clarity – knowing what you desire – and from there move straight into the mindset of courage. Rather than showing up in a relationship or at a job in the wishy-washy energy of the middle, show up with the end result energy. The energy you show up with is what creates your life. When you think as a powerful being, knowing that's who you are, knowing you are love, you manifest things immediately. Trust yourself. Trust the Universe.

When you're not trusting, you're back in the middle. When you're worrying, you're back in the middle.

A powerful tool for moving out of the middle into the end result is to constantly repeat the affirmation below. As you live in this energy, watch how everything around you shifts. Notice how empowered and confident you become. Life is so extraordinary and magical when you operate from this high vibrating energy in which everything is possible and things become simple. When you stay in the end result and believe in it, you make it happen. You create your reality. As you affirm these words, become them, feel them, believe them and receive them.

AFFIRMATION

Today and every day, I have unlimited courage.

In the Arms of an Angel

We have already touched upon the fact that there are many types of courage required of us throughout our lives and that the majority of us will find ourselves in situations in which we are asked to find an inner courage we did not know we had.

In times of difficulty, the helping hand of a friend may give us the strength we need to act bravely. However, for one young man, the helping hand of an angel literally saved the day:

Rock climbing was William's passion and he loved the challenge of it. One day in his late teens he was climbing on Ilkley Moor in Yorkshire, when he arrived at the famous Cow and Calf rocks rising above the moor itself. Unwisely he decided to scale these rocks, despite the fact that he was alone and had no ropes with him. One face of these rocks is deceptively difficult and is often used for practice climbs by some very well-known climbers.

William was halfway up the rock face when he lost his footing. One of his feet slipped from the rock and simultaneously his fingers suffered from painful cramp. He felt himself forced backwards from the rock face and in his mind's eye he could actually see his inevitable crash onto the rocks below as he began to fall. He sensed the awful loss of contact as, with only one toe still on the cliff face, he veered backwards into the void. There was simply no chance of recovery at this point and the only way was sharply down!

Suddenly, to his astonishment he felt a firm hand in the middle of his back, which pushed him back onto the rock face. The cramp left his fingers and he was able to continue upwards to safety. Amazed, he even glanced behind him, thinking for one moment that even though it seemed absolutely impossible, someone might have been behind him! Reaching the top, he vowed he would never again climb solo.

What explanation could there be, however, for the mysterious life-saving hand? William concluded that it could only have been the hand of a guardian angel, who had come to his rescue.

Always know when you have pushed beyond
your limits and bring yourself back to balance.

Leon Nacson
Dream coach and publisher

Divine Star

It takes emotional courage to look at yourself,
and to be willing to change what you aren't
happy with.

MEDITATION:
The Mountain of Courage

As well as connecting him with his guardian angel, William's mountain-top experience gave him the space in which to reconsider his attitude towards climbing – that sometimes it's wiser not to go it alone. This meditation also uses a mountain top as a place for reflection, and for manifesting one of your own desires.

As you close your eyes, take a deep breath . . . Feel your body relaxing, releasing. Inhale and exhale deeply, slowly, as you move into a space of complete relaxation.

✳ See yourself on the top of a mountain. You are already there. You have succeeded in reaching the top. Look around and notice the beauty of all that is spread out before and below you. As you take in the miracles that surround you, recognise that you are at the centre of them.

✳ Take a deep breath and affirm to yourself, 'I am courageous.' Breathe that reality in, then breathe it out to the world surrounding you. In this space of complete courage, allow yourself to have total clarity in what you feel and what you want from your life.

✳ You know what you desire. State your wish as though it has already been granted. It is already accomplished. Believe you have created it. You are in the energy of the end result, you are there now.

✳ As you look in each direction around you from your mountain top, tell everything you see that you are courageous. Explain which desire you have manifested in celebration of your courage; tell everything you see that you have accepted the end result for yourself. Notice how all that you see shifts in colour, becoming brighter, and celebrates with you.

* In this state of great courage, where else do you want to go? Where else would you like to celebrate? Is there someone you want to celebrate with? Go now to that place or that person.

* Notice as you move directly from the mountain top to your new destination that you have carried the end result with you. You are courage; you have manifested your desire. It is now a reality. As you say this in your new destination, you find that all that surrounds you begins to shift into love as well, celebrating with you.

* When the celebration feels complete, move into a space of your own, one that is nurturing and beautiful, peaceful, serene and special. In that space, know that it is real. You are courageous. You vibrate at the highest energy. You are a powerful being living in the end result. Feel the reality of it. And as you move out of this meditation, slowly, gently returning to where you are, continue to feel your new reality and affirm for yourself once more, 'I am courageous.'

AFFIRMATION

Today, I accept the extravagant abundance that is in my life. I am prosperous and give thanks for the beauty all around me.

> ⮞ *Angel Top Tip* ⮜
>
> Begin each day by taking an inventory of the
> various ways in which you can move towards
> your goals. No one is in control of your
> happiness except you; therefore, you have the
> power to change anything about yourself or
> your life that you want to change.

Seize the Day

Embrace life and banish the word 'maybe' from your thinking. Be empowered and keep motivated even when the going gets tough. The dictionary tells us that courage means bravery, fortitude and spirit, but all of these qualities can manifest in myriad ways, such as carrying on in the face of debilitating illness with cheerfulness and hope, or learning to cope after the death of a loved one, or finding the inner strength and patience to care for someone in need. All are courageous acts and require fortitude. Indeed, it sometimes requires great fortitude simply to soldier on when life seems ruled by routine and little happiness appears on the horizon.

Making the most of the opportunities that life offers us requires a certain degree of spirit, and it may sometimes seem easier to ignore the challenges that come our way and simply drift with the tide. I (Glennyce) once attended a dinner party where the conversation turned to the subject of fate and whether any of us believed in it. The guest next to me said that she firmly believed everything was down to fate and therefore there was no need for any of us to fight our destinies or try to alter our paths through life, as they had already been mapped out. It seemed to me at the time that there wasn't a great deal of spirit in her attitude to life.

I personally believe that we are presented with the choice to act upon or dismiss our options as we feel fit, and that it is the choices we make that determine our paths. Certain events, situations and people will appear in our lives, and they certainly feel as though they were 'meant to be', but we have the option of acting upon these situations or not, as the case may be.

We will of course often never know what might have happened if we had only been a little more courageous in some of our choices and attitudes. Recently, a television programme included an interview with a young woman who had been unfortunate enough to have had both hands sliced from her wrists in an industrial accident. The amazing skills of the surgeon had reattached the woman's hands very successfully and, after she had spent a long time recuperating, they were virtually fully functioning again. The reporter asked her how she had coped, if she had wondered why this had happened to her and how depressed she had been. The young woman beamed and said, 'I have never experienced depression about the situation, never had the thought "why me" – there are so many people with worse things to cope with.' She mentioned that in the hospital bed opposite hers was a woman who had lost both her legs. 'She required far more bravery than me,' said this remarkable young woman. A bright, cheerful mother of three small children, she was the very epitome of bravery, fortitude and spirit.

You cannot be brave if you've only had
wonderful things happen to you.

Mary Tyler Moore
Actress

Julie's Broken Ring

Whilst most of us would agree with Mary Tyler Moore that we can only be brave if we've experienced something to be brave about, the bravery of some of us is tested to extremes. Indeed, the courage asked of some people is astonishing. We may wonder how we will rise to life's greatest challenges, trusting we will cope if necessary, but it is only when life actually demands such bravery of us that we find out:

Life turned upside down for Julie one spring evening when she joined friends for dinner. Happily chatting and catching up on news, she was suddenly startled by her mobile phone ringing. It was her husband, David, explaining that he was feeling very unwell and heading for home after a game of squash. Julie agreed to leave immediately and head for home herself. Saying a hasty farewell to her friends, she drove home as quickly as possible, but nothing could have prepared her for the events that followed.

Walking into their lounge, she discovered that her husband had died from a heart attack. Numb with shock, she spent the following days making arrangements for the funeral, contacting friends and dealing with the paperwork relating to the tragedy. Julie spent week after week in a haze; her mind simply couldn't grasp what had happened, as is so often the case in these circumstances.

Julie and David had been married for thirty-two years and his death left a huge void in Julie's life. However, theirs was Julie's second marriage. When she was only in her teens, Julie had a boyfriend who had bought her a pretty little Victorian ring one day, which she loved and had placed on her little finger, where she had worn it ever since. Some years later the couple had married and had a daughter. Unfortunately this marriage was not to last and after their divorce Julie had had very little to do with her first husband. Many years passed and although Julie's daughter, Lisa, was still in contact with her father, he and Julie lived separate lives.

Shortly after David died, Lisa told her mother that her first husband was ill. Only a short time after receiving this news, Julie woke one morning to find her hand covered in blood. Confused as to the source of it, she went to the bathroom to wash the blood away. There she discovered that the pretty little Victorian ring, which had been on her finger for forty-five years, had broken in half and pierced her skin. Moments later the phone rang; it was her daughter Lisa with the news that her father, Julie's ex-husband, had died during the night! How astonishing that the ring should have remained on her finger for all those years, only to break the night her ex-husband died.

A little while later, Julie learnt of her first husband's bravery during those last few days. He had been given a choice of a possibly long, protracted death or switching off his pacemaker, allowing him to die peacefully and quickly. He chose the latter and spent what little time he had left talking peacefully with his family and saying his goodbyes. It was a very courageous decision, leading to a dignified death.

Trying to come to terms with these events has not been easy for Julie. She accepts that life will never be the same for her again, but knows that she must move on, and is more determined than ever to make the very best of her time with her family and friends. All this takes a very special kind of courage.

Courage is the price that life exacts for granting peace.

Amelia Earhart
US aviator (1898–1937)

The Courage to Stay the Course

Courage can take the form of action, such as climbing a mountain, tackling an assailant, speaking out or walking into a potentially difficult situation. But it can also take the form of a special kind of resilience, in which we refuse to give up and remain determined to see a situation through.

It can be particularly difficult to feel courageous when we find ourselves in circumstances beyond our immediate control, and at these times it takes a certain type of fortitude to remain optimistic, even if we know we have the support and goodwill of others. Watching someone else suffer or struggle can be a particularly heart-wrenching experience, especially if that someone is a well-loved relative or little child, as in our next story.

Ask for help.

Receiving is an act of generosity.

Cheryl Richardson
Personal coach, lecturer and author

The Perfect Sign

The marvels of modern science frequently leave us breathless and awestruck. Scientists, researchers and doctors truly appear to be miracle workers when we consider what they have achieved. Transplants, DNA profiling and micro surgery, to name but a few scientific innovations, have transformed the way we live.

Perhaps the most amazing area of change, however, is that surrounding the problems associated with premature births. A moral maze often surrounds such births. With their expertise and modern technology, medical staff are able to save the lives of premature babies earlier and earlier. It is, however, a worrying and distressing time for the parents of such infants, who are kept daily on tenterhooks as they watch their tiny babies fight for survival. Fiona and Andrew know first hand exactly how this feels.

Three years ago, Thomas was born six weeks premature and, if this was not enough of a complication, he also had heart problems that required surgery. Fiona and Andrew were beside themselves with worry and virtually never left their little boy's side for weeks. Slowly the situation began to improve until the day arrived when Thomas was strong enough to undergo surgery.

Emotions were high as the tiny child was wheeled away. The grandparents joined the anxious couple, trying to give them support and encouragement. Fiona said all they could do was to wait and pray. 'I prayed that God would give me the courage to face those dark hours,' she admitted. Eventually they received word from the theatre that the operation was going well and in its final stages. This should have been a huge relief but it was difficult to switch off the intense worry they had endured.

The first twenty-four hours after surgery would be critical and, even though their little boy was obviously a fighter, his parents sat throughout the night watching his every breath. As dawn broke, Fiona left Thomas's side for a moment to stretch her legs. Deciding she would find some coffee to keep herself and husband awake, she walked down several corridors, heading for a reception room.

Gazing out of the window in the deserted reception area, she found herself appealing to the angels for help. Silently she asked that baby Thomas's guardian angel would be with him and pull him through this pivotal time. 'Please may we have a sign,' she added, 'to know that we are not alone.' At this point, a huge, red, heart-shaped balloon floated past the window, and Fiona caught her breath. Quickly she ran through the door to see where it had come from. There was not a soul in sight, which was odd enough for an entrance to a busy city hospital. Looking upwards, she saw the balloon float up past the building and into the sky. 'Could this have been my sign?' she asked herself; it seemed too much of a coincidence that the balloon should appear apparently out of nowhere and be red and heart-shaped!

Purchasing the coffee from a nearby machine, she hurried back to her family, a feeling of optimism rising inside her. Her husband was standing by the cot when she arrived, accompanied by a doctor and nurse. All were smiling broadly. 'He is doing very well,' the doctor said. 'We feel most encouraged by his condition.' At that moment, Fiona knew for certain that the angels had heard her and answered in an appropriate and uplifting manner.

AFFIRMATION

Today, I see angels everywhere! God smiles out at me from the many symbols of courage and faith.

Jane's Dilemma

We do not have to be in a life or death situation to experience feelings of helplessness and despair. Everyday events can leave us feeling frustrated and anxious, and may require a certain amount of courage from us so that we don't crumble in the face of our problems. In these circumstances too we can benefit from calling on our angels for help, as Jane and Chloe's story shows.

At the tender age of eighteen months, Chloe was a delight.

She was a smiling, friendly little girl who was loved by all who knew her. One day in early spring, Chloe was sitting in the middle of the rug in the comfortable lounge, playing with her toys. Jane, her busy mum, was bustling around completing household tasks, including doing the wash. The noise of the washing machine suddenly ceased and Jane went into the kitchen to take the wet washing out and place more inside. One item she took from the machine was a much loved cot blanket belonging to Chloe and it occurred to her that it would be a good idea to get this dry as quickly as possible. Chloe would not be too happy if it was not on her cot that night. Peeping into the lounge to check on her daughter, she saw that she was engrossed in her play and decided to quickly run into the garden to hang the blanket on the washing line. This would ensure speedy drying in the brisk breeze. Securing the blanket with wooden pegs, Jane walked quickly back to the kitchen door, having been outside for only a moment.

To Jane's horror, the back door of her little cottage would not open. The door was of a heavy, old-fashioned, wooden type. Turning the handle in panic, Jane suddenly realised that the large iron bolt at the bottom of the door was in place and this was why she could not open it. Peeping through the kitchen window, she saw to her horror that Chloe had managed to slide the bolt across into the metal groove. Seeing her mother through the window, the little girl began to cry loudly and Jane began to panic. What on earth could she do? She noted that the window was also locked from the inside, preventing another means of entry.

Calming down a little, she tried to talk her daughter into releasing the bolt, telling her to pull it back again. Chloe did not understand and began to wail even louder. The cottage stood alone at the end of a short track and Jane was loath to leave her daughter while she went to seek help. Something had to be done, but what? Covering her eyes momentarily, she asked her guardian angel to help, pleading with her to find a solution to this distressing situation.

By this point Chloe had stopped crying, but looked terribly shocked and pale-faced as she sat in the middle of the kitchen floor. Once more Jane approached the heavy wooden door and tried to turn the handle. Instantly, the door opened wide! The heavy bolt had somehow miraculously slipped out of its moorings. Rushing inside, she hugged her little girl tight and calmed her, telling her everything was alright, Mummy was back again.

When calm had been restored and Jane had made herself a welcome cup of tea and Chloe a drink of milk, she assessed what had happened. Sliding the bolt across the bottom of the door once more, she realised that it was very easy to slide into the holding metal, but far too difficult for a little girl to slide out again. There was no way that Chloe could ever have done it, even if she had understood what was required. How, then, did the bolt become released? There was, she concluded, only one explanation possible: help had arrived that morning in the form of her angel. Jane had summoned the courage to ask for help and to this day she has the courage to defend this explanation no matter what others may say.

❧ *Angel Top Tip* ❧

Put your complete faith in the angels; ask for help and they will not fail you. No task is too small, no problem considered insignificant: you will be answered with love.

The Courage of Your Convictions and Cosmic Ordering

A type of courage we all struggle with from time to time is the courage of our own convictions. For instance, we may believe deep down that we will receive the help we need from the spiritual world, but when it actually comes to acting upon this belief we may find that we waver.

There are many books available today about a type of self-help known as 'cosmic ordering'. Cosmic ordering is the belief that a person relates his or her deepest desires to the Cosmos, which then fulfils those desires. The books and the system rose to public prominence in the UK through the television presenter Noel Edmonds, who stated very publicly that his 'cosmic list' changed his life. First published in the US, a book called *The Secret* also describes the same principle. However, we would state that there is nothing new in the concept of Cosmic Ordering. In reaching out to the angels, as humans have been doing for thousands of years, we are contacting a higher power for help, so cosmic ordering really relates to asking the angels, albeit by another name! Asking your own particular 'higher power' or 'inner angel' will achieve the same results.

Many world faiths teach these principles. Matthew and Mark, the disciples of Jesus, wrote thousands of years ago in their gospels that Jesus said 'ask and it shall be given unto you'. The only requirement is that we truly believe this help will be forthcoming.

Always anticipate the best outcome for yourself and others.

Leon Nacson
Dream coach and publisher

Yes, There Really is a Parking Angel!

When it comes to Cosmic Ordering and getting our wishes met by the Universe, you may already be aware of the stories about 'the parking angel'. Finding a free parking space may seem like a trivial request but it often represents a desperate need. Let Glennyce explain:

I was conducting a workshop recently when a young lady told me about the times she had asked her angel for a parking space and how she had always been rewarded with one.

With a look of something important dawning in her mind, a young woman called Christina, sitting close by, said that she had been to the hospital recently to visit her seriously ill mother and that she had been desperately worried there wouldn't be a parking space available. Silently, almost automatically, she had asked for a space to appear. Immediately, at the very front entrance of the hospital, a car reversed out of a space and a man appeared, waving her into the space and in effect keeping it open for her. She had never, until that moment, connected the two – her silent plea and a space appearing.

Another woman asked which hospital this had been, and when she heard which one it was she explained that she was sure the man in question had been a parking angel. She added that she had heard of many people in similar situations who described such a man stepping forward and helping them into a space when they were in dire need of one. The man always vanished, and no one inside or outside the hospital recognised the description of him, yet he appeared there time and time again.

Divine Star

Definitions of angels range from 'an immortal spiritual being attendant upon God', to 'a kind and loveable person'. You too can be an angel in someone else's life.

The Parking Angel in Hollywood

Gary and I were driving along a main road in Hollywood, hurrying as best we could to reach an appointment on time. We had arranged to meet a man at a particular restaurant. He had a very remarkable story to share and we knew he had driven a long way to meet us. However, it was now the rush hour and the traffic was becoming increasingly heavy and impossible to cut through.

We still had some way to drive down the main road before turning into the street where we were to park. Gary, being a native of this area, sighed and said that at this time of day the side street would most likely be chock-a-block with cars and we would have no chance of finding a parking space.

Suddenly we both exclaimed how here we were, advising people to trust their angels, yet we weren't asking for help ourselves. On the count of three we said in unison, 'Please, angels, may we have a parking space?' The traffic appeared to speed up a little, and, with only minutes to spare, we reached the road in which we were to meet our new friend.

Turning the corner, we smiled to see just one spare parking space, right next door to the restaurant we were heading for. Pulling in and saying a thank-you to our angels, we leapt from Gary's car. Looking up, however, we both started to laugh, because the window directly in front of us had a huge angel painted on it. In fact, we had parked in front of the 'Angel Gym'!

This taught Gary and me a valuable lesson: if we have the courage of our own convictions we will certainly be rewarded. In short, if we believe we will receive!

Have faith during inevitable conflict.

You never know how something will turn out.

Christine Northrup M.D.
Doctor and author

EXERCISE:
Stand Up and Be Counted

Do you dare act on the courage of your own convictions? What do you believe in? What you feel strongly about? What do you care about? Take a moment to think about the things in life that rattle your cage and that make you want to speak out.

If nothing immediately comes to mind, look through a newspaper or listen to the news. What makes you angry? What wrong do you wish you could right? And what are you going to do about it?

* Today, you are going to begin to change the world. How big or how small an action you take is going to be completely up to you. But you are going to do *something* ...

* If you are angry about the state of the environment, you can join a local action group; organise a group of neighbours to help tidy up the streets where you live; or simply make a resolution to recycle your household rubbish, sorting out the cans, newspapers and plastic bottles etc.

* If you are outraged by war, you can write to a prominent politician or a newspaper, stating your views; or take part in a radio phone-in; or make your own home a combat-free zone!

* If you want to take action against poverty and famine, look at ways that you can contribute by helping out in charity shops; collecting money for your favourite cause; or simply cutting down on your own extravagance and donating a little to charity each month.

* You can make a difference. All you have to do is take that first baby-step, stand up and be counted. Act on the courage of your convictions right now.

Be open, honest and honourable in all your endeavours, establish high standards, principles and values for yourself, then kick it up a level.

In everything you do be true to you.

Tavis Smiley
Talkshow host, journalist and author

> ## ✎ *Angel Top Tip* ✐
>
> Start each week with a time sheet. Add areas in
> your life where you may be able to make a
> difference. Then write in each day a space for
> yourself. As the weeks progress make that
> space a little larger until you have whole
> sections of 'me time'.

The Courage to Dare

Sometimes it takes a great deal of trust to leap into the
unknown. It may be much more comfortable to choose the
safe path, but unless we are prepared to take risks now and
again we often risk missing out on the most exciting things
in life.

It can be all too easy to ignore the ways in which you can
influence the situation you are in, deciding instead that there
is nothing you can do about it and that fate has dictated that
it will be so.

When confronted with a dilemma, try asking your angels
for guidance; they may just have placed the choice before you
in the first place! Meditate and concentrate. We have all experienced that inner 'knowing' – a feeling inside that indicates
the right way to go. You will know instinctively that this is
your angel's answer. How often do you ignore this inner voice,
only later to say to yourself, 'I knew I should not have done
that'? It is common to us all. Have the courage to believe that
your inner voice may be your inner angel leading you gently
in the right direction.

Pick up the pace of your life,

add a new activity, make a new acquaintance,

read a new book, or take a new course,

move outside your everyday mundane existence,

add a new beat and expand your boundaries.

Tavis Smiley

Comfort and Courage from the Angels

Sometimes courage takes different forms in different situations. Margaret and her husband are a good example of this.

Years ago at the height of the Troubles, Margaret had to say goodbye to her husband, knowing that he would be travelling to Ireland where he might find himself in some very dangerous situations. Although he would be the one facing danger while Margaret remained behind in England, Margaret needed courage to face each day in the knowledge that her husband's life was under threat.

As so often happens in such circumstances, Margaret was finding it extremely difficult to sleep. The minute she put her head to the pillow her mind started to work overtime. One night as she lay there, quite exhausted because of lack of sleep and yet still unable to drift off, she heard a voice saying, 'Do not worry, he'll be fine.' Without a second thought, Margaret knew instinctively that this was her guardian angel and she fell at once into a deep sleep. The angel's message was correct because her husband was indeed fine.

The thought that she had a guardian angel was often in Margaret's mind from that day on and she derived a lot of comfort from it. Some years later Margaret exhibited another form of courage by deciding to become a mature student at university. Studying would not be easy and she knew she would have to work very hard, secretly wondering if in fact she was up to the challenge.

Early in the course she found herself chatting to a fellow student and the conversation turned to the subject of angels. It appeared that the young woman was a firm believer in angels and Margaret found her a comforting companion on the course. However, as time passed Margaret began to feel her courage and self-belief waver dramatically. Daily she tussled with the idea that maybe she was not really up to academic work. Once they had crept into her mind her doubts began to multiply and she found herself in a state of turmoil. (When telling us her story, Margaret stressed the word 'turmoil', saying it was the only word that accurately described her feelings at that time.) As she mulled over the possibility that maybe she didn't have the required ability, her spirits started on a downward spiral.

One morning, on waking, she simply did not want to get out of bed. Negative thoughts filled her head and she was terribly frustrated. Forcing herself to sit bolt upright in bed she said aloud, 'OK – if I have a guardian angel, please give me a sign.' Feeling better for having asked, she got out of bed and dressed for the day.

After breakfast, she switched on her computer and there to her amazement was an e-mail from one of her tutors. The tutor was asking Margaret if she might use one of her assignments as a model for another student. She said the work was excellent and would be of great benefit to her new students! Could there have been greater proof that Margaret's work was indeed acceptable and that Margaret was more than up to the task? Knowing for certain this was the sign she had only moments before asked her angel for, Margaret thanked her guardian angel for such a swift response! She no longer entertains ideas of abandoning her course, nor doubts her academic ability. However, the one thing she is most certain of after this incident is the fact that her guardian angel is ever near and constantly listening.

AFFIRMATION

*Today, I release anything within me
that seeks to block my greater good
from manifesting.*

*Remember that life is very simple, you create
your experiences by your thinking and feeling
patterns.*

Louise L. Hay
Author and publisher

EXERCISE:
Have the Courage to be Kind to Yourself

When we stray away from our familiar routines in the way
that Margaret did by becoming a mature student, the experience can often be strange and unsettling at first. In fact,
we may feel guilty if we find that we are enjoying ourselves
by doing something for ourselves rather than out of duty
for someone else.

One area of life that takes courage is the ability to have
fun. Your initial reaction may be, why should that take
courage? Well, believe it or not, many people are simply
afraid to have fun. For them, just letting go, letting their
hair down and enjoying themselves seems impossible.

Psychologists, physicians and theologians all recommend
a good laugh to make one feel better. It is well documented
that if we laugh more our physical and psychological problems will be lessened. Our general health will improve and

in fact statistics reveal that we actually live longer if we laugh a lot! It is perfectly OK to be silly even if only from time to time; it will add quality to your life. You may need to indulge in a good face cream to keep the laughter lines under control, but that is a small price to pay for feeling good! Rope your friends or family in and do something just because it is fun. If you have a strong sense of duty you may find that fun is very low on your list of priorities. Work of one kind or another will be dominating your life. Do not let this happen. Start this moment and book a day off, ring a friend and arrange to do something relaxing and lovely that will bring fun into both your lives. Make a list of activities you love but have neglected to do for some time. Promise yourself you will work down the list. You may wish to start with something very small and work your way up to some very serious fun indeed! Here are a few suggestions to get you off to a flying start:

1. Go for 'afternoon tea' and order jam and scones or a large piece of chocolate cake.

2. Learn a new joke and repeat it to your friends or neighbours.

3. Go into your nearest city, sit in a coffee shop, daydream and watch the world go by.

4. Visit the cinema with friends.

5. Go for a swim. And if you can't swim, enrol in lessons!

6. Take a day trip to the seaside and make a sand castle.

7. Book a full day at a spa. Indulge in every treatment on offer!

8. Treat yourself to some beautiful flowers.

9. Get the old bike out from the garage and go for a spin.

10. Try a new hairstyle, or even change the colour!

11. Take a dog for a stroll or spend five minutes stroking a

cat. (If you don't own one, borrow a friend's pet.)

12. Buy a plant or sow some seeds. Talk to your plant as it grows.

13. Sit on a park bench with a favourite book.

14. Go down the slide in that park!

> *Learning to stop is the first step on the road back to sanity.*

Edward England
Writer

Time to Be Brave

Be courageous enough to slow down and alter the pace of your life, if only for one day a week. It's not selfish behaviour: you deserve time to step back and assess what is really necessary for you. There may be times when it feels as if the window of inspiration has a curtain drawn over it. If you slow down a little it may give you a chance to draw that curtain back and let the light in.

Each human life has a finite time on earth, so we owe it to ourselves, and indeed to our creator, to use that time wisely. Have you always longed to have time to be more creative yet regarded this concept as frivolous? How often do you meet up with your friends and just laugh, often for no reason at all, just for the sheer joy of being together? Have you passed up on some opportunity because you tell yourself that you are too busy? All the time you know in your heart that you should have had the courage to 'go for it' and step out of your comfort zone . . .

Look for things to feel good about, and watch how everything in your life will unfold to reflect that good feeling vibration.

Abraham-Hicks
Channeller

The Rewards of Being Courageous

For Helen the saying 'stepping out of your comfort zone' had a very literal meaning:

Everything that could possibly go wrong in Helen's life had gone wrong. A long-term relationship had reached an abrupt end, and then her employer announced that the company was in trouble and would be closing down, leaving Helen with no income. To say that Helen was at a very low ebb would be a huge understatement; she was quite at a loss as to what to do next. Not wishing to worry her family, she confided in friends near and far, even discussing her predicament with a good friend in New Zealand via the internet. Talking about the problem helped a little as her friends were very sympathetic, but they were unable to offer any concrete support.

A few weeks later, Helen was astonished to receive a phone call from her friend Susan in New Zealand. Susan explained that there was the offer of a job in her business, should Helen wish to take it, and she added how happy she and her family would be to welcome Helen to their lovely part of the world. Leaving England was an option that would never have occurred to Helen and she was in complete shock at the idea.

Promising to think about it, she thanked Susan and spent a sleepless night pondering the possibility of such a move. Eventually, after several days of mulling it over, Helen thought, 'Nothing ventured, nothing gained!' It was the perfect opportunity to take life by the scruff of the neck. She knew the move would take a great deal of courage and that her nerve might falter many times along the way, but she rang Susan nevertheless and accepted her offer.

Five years later, Helen is back in England. She enjoyed life to the full in New Zealand and spent her time there very happily, making new friends and learning new skills. Returning home, she found her new expertise and experience guaranteed her the sort of employment she could have only dreamed about before leaving.

By taking up Susan's job offer, Helen had in every sense left her comfort zone, which had taken great courage, especially for Helen who was in fact a rather shy person. She has, however, been amply rewarded for her courageous actions.

The key to happiness is realising that it's not what happens to you that matters, it's how you choose to respond.

Keith D. Harrell
Professional speaker and author

Let Your Starlight Shine!

It is time to give yourself a 'life review' to discover what course of action you could take to express your latent talents and fulfil your true potential. Don't let your light stay hidden under that bushel, let it shine! Hidden talents are of no use to anyone, especially not to you, so bring them out, dust them off, enjoy them and let others enjoy them too.

There are so many things in life to try. How many of us have held a secret desire to ride a horse, learn to swim, or camp out under the stars? Sometimes we may feel these exciting activities may be beyond us, either financially or time-wise. However, if we are serious about living life to the full, we can always find ways around the obstacles in our way. Do it *now* – don't let the moment pass! In your Angel Journal, write down a dozen activities that interest you. Now, choose one of them and pursue it . . . Be courageous, kick your heels and let the dust settle a little if you need to; your old life will still be there if you want it when you get home! Give yourself a little respect and have the courage to believe in your own judgement when you set out on your new adventure.

Now is the time to take direct action in your life, your thinking and your outlook. It takes courage to break old habits and patterns that we have adhered to for most of our life. Consciously banish the thoughts that drain you, such as 'I can't . . .', 'what will so-and-so think . . .', 'I'm too old', 'I haven't the time to . . .'

Identify areas that can be simplified in your workplace or home. Are you spending far too much time on inconsequential duties? Take a look: there will be many small tasks that have gradually built up into major tasks, clogging your time each day. When someone asks you to do yet another tiresome task, be brave and say, 'Excuse me, this life is occupied!' By making a dedicated effort the decks can truly be cleared and you can start afresh. So spring clean the workplace and your home. When you have done this, reward yourself and congratulate yourself on taking the first courageous step in your new life.

An even more effective way of making a fresh start is to encourage others to join you. Ask your work colleagues to join in the streamlining, ask your family or friends to join in with your new determined attitude and to laugh with you, to create a joyful new life. Organise time for yourself and time for others. The time you devote to others will be all the more enriched by the time you give to yourself.

Each week brings us 168 golden hours.

We spend approximately 56 hours for sleep and recuperation,

28 hours for eating and personal duties,

40–50 hours for earning a living.

We have 30–40 hours left to spend as we wish,

but how do we spend them?

Anon

EXERCISE:
Fearful Thinking vs. Courageous Thinking

Are you ready to take charge of your life and embrace the future? Let's discover what your current beliefs are and if they have changed since you started working with the exercises in this book. This exercise can be repeated as many times as you wish to uncover the hidden patterns of thinking that influence your life.

You will need:

a friend or partner (who is a good listener and who will offer no judgements or comments)

a pen and paper (e.g. Angel Journal)

STEP 1

Your partner asks you: what is your greatest fear about your life and/or the situation you are currently in?

You reply out loud: _____

Your partner asks you: what would you like to change about your life and/or current situation?

You reply out loud: _____

When you partner has isolated the key elements of the situation or your life circumstances as you understand them, your partner writes them down for you here or in your Angel Journal:

_____

_____

STEP 2

Once you have identified the key elements of your situation, your partner asks you the following questions:

Partner: what are the beliefs that are creating this situation?

You reply: _____

Partner: what experiences are reinforcing those beliefs and creating certainty in those beliefs, do you think?

You reply: _____

Partner: What beliefs might someone else have in order to experience a similar situation?

*You reply:*_____

STEP 3

Answer the following questions by writing each answer down and then reading them aloud to your partner. Be fearless:

1. What beliefs might lead YOU to be a success in life?

_____

2. What beliefs might lead YOU to live a life of abundance and courage?

_____

3. What beliefs might lead YOU to trust the Universe and live in the truth of the magic of spiritual reality?

_____

Have your partner read your statements from Step 3 back to you. Listen to them; accept them as truths and believe in their validity in your own life. Know now that you are one with the Universe and at this moment you accept Peace, Love and Courage in your life.

Be Bold, Be Brave, Be Beautiful!

You too have the ability to do whatever frightens you. You don't have to be a superhero or possessed of extraordinary strength or talent. It sometimes takes more courage to make little changes than it does to tackle a crisis, but little changes can lead to some big improvements. The winds of change will blow freshly through all areas of your life if only you allow them to. Welcome in a gentle breeze and it may even become a gale, blowing away all that clutter and rubbish! Try not to be afraid; most of the time there is nothing to fear but fear itself. Assess exactly what it is that causes you such anxiety, and realise that your fear of doing anything you find daunting will frequently be dispelled by your actually doing it!

Take your courage in both hands and go out to face the day. This is your life, not a rehearsal. The world is a beautiful place, people are wonderful, so enjoy everything that's out there. That said, life isn't always easy and you may need to draw upon your inner resources to face the challenges ahead; in which case you can rest assured that your angels will support you through the hard times whenever you need them. So be brave; it's time to claim the happiness that can be yours.

Feel the fear and do it anyway.

Dr Susan Jeffers
Author and public speaker

**STAR POINTS TO
PONDER:**

I am taking up a new activity.

I can say 'no' with a smile.

I recognise my fear and move on.

I ask others for help when necessary.

I give myself the gift of time.

*I am happy to take chances and trust
my angel to take care of me.*

I am not afraid to change.

6

The Star of Peace

Let there be peace on earth

And let it begin with me;

Let there be peace on earth

The peace that was meant to be

Let peace begin with me,

Let this be the moment now

With every step I take,

Let this be my solemn vow.

Sy Miller and Jill Jackson

Today's Yearning for Peace

The Star of Peace concerns peace in all its forms. However, here we will be concentrating on the subject of inner peace and how this may be achieved.

Coping with the demands of today's busy world can be very difficult and a common expression – especially amongst the younger generation – is 'I'm so stressed!' An old lady once remarked to us that young people no longer know the meaning of hard work; she herself had toiled on a farm from a very early age. However, while long working days and hard physical work are certainly never going to be easy options, today's form of hard work is often of a cerebral kind and equally demanding.

Long periods of concentration and a heavy workload not only make us feel mentally weary but can lead to physical problems as well. Headaches, fatigue and repetitive strain injuries all contribute to a stressful lifestyle. It is very important that we find ways of relieving the stress that sometimes threatens to overpower us. Yoga, t'ai chi, meditation and walking are all beneficial activities if factored into our lives.

We have already mentioned the importance of finding 'me time' when considering the Star of Gratitude and the Star of Courage, but we would like to mention this again in relation to the key concept of inner peace. Finding true inner peace requires a dedicated effort, but without doubt it is an effort that will be rewarded.

Whatever your circumstances, whether you belong to a small or large family, a twosome or singledom, it is important for your physical and mental health to find some inner peace. When you feel relaxed and happy personally, then all other areas of your life will be in balance. You can begin by taking a few simple steps, first by simply finding a quiet spot in your home. Sit in a comfortable chair, light a candle and meditate for a while. Put a soothing piece of music on your CD player and listen carefully to the wonderful sounds and lyrics. You might simply wish to sit and daydream, gazing out of the window at nature. Over a period of time, you might extend this experience to treating yourself to a long soak in the tub, or quality time alone in the garden.

To create time to yourself, you may have to prioritise, lose some tasks or relinquish involvement in various activities and concede that you cannot do everything. Stretching ourselves in too many directions often results in our only half completing things, so it is much more beneficial to do less more competently. Consider the fact that the more peaceful and relaxed you feel, the better equipped you will be to deal with life's demands.

And remember you are not alone in this: your Angel of Peace is only too ready to help; you only have to ask, then make a space for her to come into your life and the peace you so badly need will be yours.

Every now and then, go away, have a little relaxation,

For when you come back to your own work, your judgement will be surer; since to remain constantly at work will cause you to lose power of judgement.

Leonardo da Vinci
Artist and inventor (1452–1519)

Divine Star

When we come to earth we have the help and encouragement of our angels and spirit guides. Everyone has angels and guides. Some have the same guide throughout their lives. Souls that are allowed to be guided are usually more evolved.

AFFIRMATION

Today, I am at peace.

You work that you may keep peace with the earth and the soul of the earth.

Kahlil Gibran
Artist, poet and writer (1883–1931)

A Little Bird Told Her!

Trisha's lovely tale reveals the importance of finding a little personal space or a haven in which to find inner peace. Once we have found inner peace, we can begin to reassess our options:

'One would be hard pressed to find a more idyllic setting than this,' thought Trisha, staring out of the window. Holding a mug of hot coffee, she gazed out at the beautiful scene. The sea was like the proverbial mill pond and a glorious shade of – well, aquamarine actually! The deep blue sky and bright sunshine completed the lovely picture. Even though it was early February and frost tipped the leaves outside, the sun made her feel warm and cosy.

It had been a God-send of an opportunity, Trish mused. She had received an offer from two very good friends to stay in their beautiful cottage whilst they went skiing for a week and all she had to do in return was feed their three cats, a perfect arrangement. It could not have been more timely, for if there was one thing that Trisha needed it was peace and quiet and time to think. Life had certainly presented her with emotional ups and downs these past few years. Although six months had passed since Trisha's long-term relationship had broken up, it still felt very raw. And now here was an exciting new venture that scared the living daylights out of her. She had received the offer of a job abroad, a prospect that excited and scared her in equal measures. Here in this wonderful setting she had a chance to really mull over all the pros and cons and hopefully reach a decision.

Trisha's best friend, Ruth, told her to ask the angels for a sign, for some positive way of helping her make up her mind. 'It seems very unlikely,' she thought, 'that an angel would appear to me here in this little cottage, but I'll ask for a sign anyway and see what happens.' Carrying her mug of coffee outdoors, Trisha sat on the little bench beneath the kitchen window and silently asked the angels for a sign that all would be well. She was surprised to find the sun warm enough to allow her to sit there for a little while. It was so beautiful that she felt completely at peace, and all her worries simply slipped away. A sudden movement caught Trisha's eye and she saw to her delight a little robin flutter down and sit on the arm of her bench. Smiling, Trisha said to the little bird, 'You have just made my day!'

The time passed in a pleasant haze and on the second day Trisha thought she might take her sketchbook down to the shore and draw for a little while. Walking into the kitchen to make breakfast, she was delighted to see her little robin land on the windowsill and stare in at her. She had the feeling that he was looking directly into her eyes. 'I wish you could talk,' she thought to herself. 'I wonder what you want to tell me.'

Soon it was Friday and as Trisha woke in her pretty cottage bedroom, she stretched with a sigh, wishing she could make the week last a little longer. It had been a revelation having so much time to herself. She had loved every minute of it. Even the weather had been kind; the sky and sea were still a wonderful clear blue, the winter sun had not failed one single day and she felt so very fortunate. For the first time in years, she felt truly at peace with herself and the world.

Trisha took her coffee to the bench outside once more. This had become a little ritual and was the perfect way to start each day. Right on time, her robin appeared and once more settled on the arm of the bench. He had never failed to appear each morning and now he felt like an old friend. Sitting on the bench that Friday morning Trisha realised that she had in fact reached a decision. She would accept the job: 'Nothing ventured, nothing gained,' she told herself. 'These opportunities come only occasionally in life,' she mused, 'and I must seize the day.' Turning to her little robin friend, she told him of her decision and didn't feel foolish chatting to him at all!

Saturday morning dawned and Trisha packed her suitcase in readiness to leave later in the day. Her friends would be home for lunch so she planned to prepare a meal to welcome them back home. As usual, she took her coffee outdoors after breakfast but was terribly disappointed when her robin failed to arrive. 'That is so sad,' she remarked aloud. 'It'll be the last chance I have to see him.'

Her friends arrived back after a splendid holiday and they all chatted happily for some time over lunch. She was then asked if she had reached a decision. Her friends were delighted and supportive when she told them she had indeed. With a little embarrassed laugh, she then said she had asked the angels for a sign to help her but she had not seen one! 'Still, I made friends with a beautiful little robin and talked the problem over with him,' she laughed. She explained how he had visited every day at breakfast time and how she had told him of her decision yesterday. She added that sadly he had not arrived this morning to say goodbye.

Trisha noticed that her friends were looking at her in a rather strange manner. 'What?' she asked.

'Clearly,' they replied, 'you've not heard about robins being a well known sign from the angels!'

Trisha was stunned. Suddenly it all fell into place: the little bird had stayed with her until her decision had been made, and this morning he knew he was no longer required! What a revelation, she thought, as the angels had answered her in the most appropriate way. Trisha travelled home with a warm happy feeling inside and recognised her newfound calm as a sense of much-sought-after inner peace.

> *Only the open-minded can be at peace,*
>
> *For they alone see reason for it*
>
> **Little Book of Miracles**

Start Small, Think Big

If we can all achieve a little inner peace, it will be sure to have a knock-on effect on those immediately around us, and who knows where the influence will end? Indeed, many of the major peace movements in the world have been inspired by individuals. One of the key episodes of the African-American civil rights movement in the USA was sparked by Rosa Parks when she simply but firmly refused to give up her bus seat.

Similarly, the peace movement in the 1960s had humble origins but eventually had a huge effect on society. Women stood up to be counted in great numbers, wanting to ensure a peaceful future for the younger generation. The hippy flower children were 'dropping out' and saying 'peace, man' to anyone who would listen. Glennyce recalls living in San Francisco when she was young and experiencing at first hand that atmosphere of love and peace. It was only fifteen years since the end of the Second World War, and people wanted to make love, not war, and carried banners to that effect. The sixties brought such freedom to a recently oppressed world that the yearning for peace was palpable. Walking through Golden Gate Park at that time was a revelation as tents spread as far as the eye could see, like a permanent Glastonbury!

We could certainly use some of that spirit of peace in today's war-torn world. Although we seem to be living on a planet troubled by religious differences, the word 'Islam' actually means peace, as does the Hebrew word *shalom*. Christians sing about peace on earth and indeed all the world's major religions express their desire for peace. While it is unlikely that individuals speaking in isolation can persuade the many factions in world conflicts to lay down their arms simultaneously, we can make a difference in our own little corners of the world and trust our actions will spread. We may feel powerless to make a difference to the world but the fact is that if we find internal peace, we will radiate this peace to others. It will flow and grow and reach areas we never thought possible. Indeed, given the conflict that exists within our world today, every individual needs to contribute towards a more peaceful planet.

Have peace in your hearts

and thousands around you will be healed.

St Seraphim of Sarov

Divine Star

Welcome tranquillity into your life. Make your
home a haven and then learn how to spread
your newfound peace into the greater world. It
may appear to be an overwhelming idea to
start world peace all by yourself, but there was
never a more relevant time to reach towards
that goal. And once you start to think about it,
you might be surprised by the many ways in
which you too can make a difference.

EXERCISE:
A Little Taste of Peace

You don't need to go on a protest march or sign a petition
to make a stand for peace. You can start small, and spread a
little taste of peace to all your friends, family and colleagues
by treating them to these cookies.

You will need:
    250g unsalted butter, at room temperature
    140g caster sugar
    1 egg yolk
    2 tsp vanilla extract
    300g plain flour, sifted (plus more if needed)
    ½ teaspoon baking powder
    A pinch of salt
    A measure of goodwill
    1 dove-shaped or heart-shaped cookie cutter (available

from cook shops or you can make your own from
stiff card)
2 non-stick baking sheets

For the icing:
2 large egg whites
2 teaspoons fresh lemon juice
300g icing sugar, sifted
Food colouring (optional)

* Preheat the oven to 180°C/gas mark 4.

* Cream the sugar and butter together in a large bowl until
the butter looks fluffy, then beat in the egg yolk and
vanilla extract. Gradually sift the flour over the mixture
and fold it in, with the baking powder and the pinch of
salt. All the time, think positive and healing thoughts as
you mix the dough. Add a little more flour if the mix
looks too sticky to roll out.

* Sprinkle a surface with flour and then roll out the dough
so that it's about half a centimetre thick. Dip the cookie
cutter in flour (to prevent sticking) and cut the dough
into shapes. Place the cookies a little apart on the baking
sheets.

* Bake the cookies for 10 to 12 minutes, or until they have
gone golden-brown around the edges. Let them cool on
the baking sheet for a few minutes before transferring to
a wire rack.

* You can use ready-made icing if you wish. Or, if you
would like to make your own royal icing, beat the 2 large
egg whites with the lemon juice. Fold in the sifted icing
sugar and combine until smooth. Again, while you are
folding in the sugar, focus on sending positive and kind

thoughts towards everyone who is going to taste these cookies! Add a couple of drops of food colouring if you wish to have coloured icing. Use the icing immediately to decorate your cooled cookies.

✴ Once the icing is dry (which may take a couple of hours) store the cookies between sheets of grease-proof paper.

✴ Give the cookies to your friends, family and colleagues to sweeten up their day and spread a little peace and happiness!

You get world peace through inner peace.

If you've got a world of people who have inner peace, then you have a peaceful world.

Dr Wayne W. Dyer
Psychotherapist, lecturer and author

Making Every Moment Count

Global peace may seem a far-fetched goal when on a day-to-day basis so many of us struggle with anxieties, worries and doubts. The world moves at a frenetic pace and at times we struggle to keep up. Multi-tasking has in many cases become the normal way of life, especially for women. The need to travel great distances frequently, and to understand modern technology, add to the pressures of life in the twenty-first century. We worry on behalf of our children too, as there are so many activities and areas of study they are expected to be involved with. Little wonder we sometimes feel we are living on a treadmill!

Do you remember the words of the flower-power tune

'Feeling Groovy' by Simon and Garfunkel? It says, 'Slow down, you move to fast, try to make the morning last.' We could all benefit from taking that philosophy to heart. Glennyce knows someone who worked very hard indeed for her employer, even spending precious weekends at work to ensure the smooth running of her job. After twenty-five years of loyal service, she received a letter telling her that she was no longer required. There was no special thanks for all her hard work, no party, flowers, or cards to wish her well, not even a drink with colleagues; she simply emptied her desk and left. And she had no chance to regain those lost weekends or to make up the hours she had spent working late; all that time had gone for ever.

The past is gone for good and the future is a mystery – we only have now, and we have to use it wisely. The gift of time is precious, which is why it is called the present!

A Heavenly Message

Every moment is precious, however mundane, and can hold a special message for us if only we look carefully, as Stephanie discovered. Here is her story:

It is a great blessing to be very close as a family; not all families are harmonious and Stephanie would be the first to admit that she was fortunate.

As Stephanie's mother Gwendoline grew older and a little frail, it was agreed that she would go to live with Stephanie and her family. She was much loved and cared for until her very last days. Hers had been a long and happy life, full of adventure. Over the years, she had often flown to Australia to visit her younger daughter Yvonne. Now she had passed away and was greatly missed by all the family.

Stephanie found herself missing her mother terribly; they

had been great friends as well as mother and daughter. They had always had fun together, playing cards and games and thoroughly enjoying each other's company. One morning a little time after her mother's death, Stephanie woke feeling very emotional and low. She found herself talking to her mum out loud, saying, 'Oh Mum, I do miss you. How I wish there was some way I could talk to you. Do you think that at some point today you could send me a message?' It would be wonderful, she thought, to know that they could still communicate.

The day wore on and Stephanie carried on with household chores until later that afternoon she went to find her sewing box. This was kept in a cupboard containing many things that had belonged to her mother. Searching the cupboard, she was startled to see a photograph flutter to the floor. It had clearly fallen out of one of the photograph albums stored there.

It was a lovely photograph of her mother, sitting in the garden of her sister's home in Australia. She was writing at a garden table. Stephanie turned the photograph over and read the words on the back. Her mother had written 'sending a message to Stephanie'! Scarcely able to believe her eyes, Stephanie stared with amazement and sheer happiness at the very timely message. Here was the sign she had asked for that morning. Sensations of warmth surrounded her as she held the precious photograph.

Later that day Stephanie started to fit the pieces of the puzzle together. She had never seen the message on the back of the photograph before, because her mother, who always took lots of photographs on her trips to Australia, had already secured it firmly in the album. The album was of a type that had two photographs sitting back to back on one page so their reverse sides were never visible. Many times Stephanie had moved items in that cupboard and never before had this, or indeed any photograph, fallen from the album.

This was clearly not a mere coincidence but a spiritually inspired moment of synchronicity. The powerful feeling of love Stephanie felt and the succinct message left her in no doubt that this was the sign she had asked for that very day. It was as if the message had been frozen in time, only to emerge when Stephanie needed to receive it most.

> *What you dismiss as an ordinary coincidence*
> *may be an opening to an extraordinary*
> *adventure.*
>
> **Deepak Chopra M.D.**
> Doctor and spiritual teacher

Angels, Signs and Coincidences

Angels will utilise virtually any medium in order to contact us in the most appropriate way. For Stephanie, longing for a sign that day, the photograph of her mother was full of special meaning. However, telephones, televisions sets and even computers have all been involved with messages and signs. It is as if the angels are waiting for us to catch up with their expertise.

Unfortunately many of us fail to recognise these signs and so the angelic connection is not realised. However, as we have seen, when we trust that we have been given a sign we frequently start a chain reaction and others will appear, especially when we ask for them.

We may find ourselves thinking 'I wonder if it could be the angels . . .' when something in our lives appears to be out of the ordinary and often if we simply trust it to be a sign, more than likely it will be. Angelic communications can take so many forms, such as a fragrance with no discernible source that reminds us of a particular person we are thinking about. This fragrance could be perfume, cigar smoke or a completely unidentifiable scent that is difficult to describe but wonderful to experience. Maybe we feel the touch of a hand, a caress on the head, or the sensation of arms encircling us when we are alone. We might experience a bright light, which could be white or coloured. Or, most commonly of all, the angels may communicate to us through a form of a coincidence.

Of all the various types of angelic intervention, coincidences are perhaps the most intriguing. Virtually everyone has experienced a memorable coincidence at some point in their lives. Sadly, we may often dismiss these as literally 'mere coincidences', instead of looking more deeply at the phenomenon.

Coincidences are often described as a random series of events in an ordered life, often surprising in nature and varying from the simplest to the most dramatic. We feel, however, that the opposite is true: coincidences often represent an ordered set of events in a chaotic life. How many times have we thought about a friend whom we have not seen for years, only to bump into them a few moments later? Likewise, we may think about a well-known song that is significant in our life and, as we turn on the radio, it will be playing. If we look deeper and ask what we are being told by these events, the answers may surprise us.

Coincidences are often part of a larger pattern that is being brought to our attention for a purpose. A series of coincidences or a 'cluster' (to use a phrase coined by the famous Austrian biologist Paul Kammerer) is even more indicative that we should take notice of what is happening. In circumstances involving a series of coincidences, it's not unusual to hear someone say, 'It was meant to be.' Indeed it was. We may ignore these messages, of course, and possibly miss out on the most amazing opportunity of our lives. We all have free choice. However, it would be well worth giving the angels a chance and looking a little more closely at the coincidences in your own life.

Divine Star

Angels are literally 'the light of your life'.
Allow them to shine and bring their light into
even your darkest corners.

Bernard's Little Miracle

Bernard's story shows that angels can appear in our lives when
and where we least expect them, taking coincidence to a
higher level:

Just three days after her ninetieth birthday Bernard's mother
died. Happiness was mixed in with the sadness of her passing,
especially for Bernard. He had travelled from the United States
of America for his mother's special birthday and the whole
family had enjoyed the special occasion. It was the first time
in many years that the entire extended family had been
together. Moreover, Bernard had had many long chats with
his mother in the days before her birthday and he was grateful
for that. The funeral was a bitter-sweet occasion, as everyone
delighted that she had enjoyed a wonderful time immediately
prior to her death.

On the morning Bernard and his wife were due to leave for
the airport to fly back home, his sister asked if he would like
to take an item or two of his mother's belongings with them.
He refused, saying just a photograph would be sufficient.
However, sometime later when Bernard had had time to
reflect, he regretted his decision to refuse an item as a
keepsake. This was mainly because he recalled the lovely
antique clock he had bought his mother for her sixtieth
birthday. She had had a passion for clocks, especially antique

ones, and though she did not have a large collection, the ones she possessed were very special to her. She had told Bernard on many occasions how much she loved this particular little clock. It was a rather unusual shape, delicate and beautifully embellished with one or two precious stones.

'I really should have asked for that clock,' Bernard said to himself sadly, but it would be too late now. Her home had been cleared, of that he was sure. His mother's home had been a large, rambling house, full of old furniture and artefacts that her children had no desire to keep. His sisters had therefore organised a house clearance and Bernard learned to his dismay that his mother's precious clocks had been included in this transaction.

Several years had passed when Bernard and his wife received a wedding invitation for his niece's wedding that summer. They were delighted and eagerly looked forward to the trip. It would be lovely to catch up with everyone again under happy circumstances.

In the event the day was wonderful, the bride beautiful and the weather perfect. A few days after the wedding, Bernard and his wife hired a car to tour around Britain for a holiday before returning home.

Driving one morning through a lovely village in Suffolk, they stopped for lunch in a delightful thatched tea room. Later they took a stroll around the scenic little village, popping into shops to buy gifts for friends back home. They came across an antique shop and went inside, gazing with wonder at the myriad nick-nacks for sale. Every nook was piled high with interesting articles. Browsing with pleasure, suddenly Bernard came to a halt and shouted to his wife to come and look at what he had found. They both stood and stared open-mouthed at the item in Bernard's hand: it was his mother's clock! It was the very clock he had bought her all those years ago and that he had believed to be lost for ever. Here they were in a village two hundred miles away from his family home and in a shop crammed with goods.

'I simply cannot believe it,' Bernard said. 'This is a little miracle.'

'More like a little angel,' said his wife 'Only an angel could have led you here today!' Few people would disagree.

Divine Star

Our thoughts attract the conditions and events that we experience in our lives; the conditions that we think about and activate correspond exactly to our mental state. Thought is therefore not only about latent power; it also determines the form of all things. So start to focus on thoughts of happiness, inspiration, courage, care and the support of all others. In grace, love and gratitude, begin to create an inner and outer manifestation of peace.

Tap into the unlimited mind of creation and draw from it the right plans and actions that will lead you to your ultimate success.

Keith D. Harrell
Professional speaker and author

Welcome to Paradise

As in Bernard's story about his mother's clock, it often seems that when we talk about peace, we refer in the same breath to those who are near death or those who are actually dying.

We all hope that those we love will experience a peaceful end to their lives, and indeed that we will too. From our research into true encounters with angels, it appears that accounts of deceased loved ones and angels visiting those close to death are on the increase. It may, however, simply be the case that these events were always frequent, but that people were once more reluctant to discuss them openly than they are today.

Science and spirituality have often been at loggerheads, but after years of research many more scientists are beginning to accept the validity of deathbed revelations that refer to angels or spiritual encounters. More than twenty-five years have gone by since Dr Raymond Moody first published his wonderful book about near-death experiences, *Life after Life*, which was thought revolutionary when it first appeared. In 1969, Dr Elisabeth Kübler Ross published her ground-breaking book *Death and Dying*, which allowed for a spiritual dimension, and when the Dutch general practitioner Dr Hans C. Moolenburgh published his findings, he included research into angelic appearances as reported by his patients. Encouraged by this, there is a much more open attitude now than there was thirty or forty years ago, which means that more of us are coming forward to discuss our experiences and the experiences of our loved ones close to death.

Modern-day research has even identified a pattern of events in the days leading up to a person's death. The research concludes that one or two days before the person passes away he or she will see a loved one who has passed away some time before. This is almost always someone who had been very close to that person in life, and who represents a loving and comforting presence. Such a visitation must reassure the dying person that he or she will be looked after and led into the next world by someone very dear. Research has also recorded sightings of a light or a white mist rising from the newly deceased body. This light or mist often lingers for some time and has been witnessed by relatives and nursing staff.

So it would appear that science is at long last catching up with the spiritual. Continuing scientific investigations are sure to reveal many more comforting facts about those approaching death. We may even reach the point where encountering a person in spirit or an angel (and they may be the same thing) is considered normal in such circumstances. What a wonderfully comforting thought that would be and it would truly lead to peace of mind for us all!

However, we do not necessarily need scientific evidence of life after death, as I (Glennyce) found out one morning. I was sharing a car with Gordon Smith, who is one of Britain's most loved and spookily accurate mediums. We were both on our way to the Independent Television studios in London, where we were to take part in a debate on the television show 'This Morning'. As we drove through the busy traffic, we chatted to the driver of the car as well as to each other. Recognising Gordon, the driver was full of questions and all three of us became engaged in a debate about the afterlife. As we got out of the car when we arrived at the studios we both said goodbye to our driver, but the parting words to him from Gordon were: 'Listen, you cannot die, even if you want to!' Words to ponder on indeed . . .

Wendy's Angel

In the Star of Harmony we told you about the funeral of Wendy's mother. Here we are going to share with you a remarkable event that took place just twenty-four hours before Wendy lost her mum:

Setting out directly from work on Friday evening, Wendy began the long journey to her mother's house. She was feeling distressed and anxious, aware how poorly her mother was at this point. Wendy's mother had been ill with cancer for a very long time and, although periods of remission had given the family hope, eventually she became terminally ill despite everyone's best efforts. So there was Wendy, driving on a cold dark December night, fearful of what she might find on her arrival. Inside, she churned with thoughts and feelings of what lay ahead and how she would cope with the worst scenario.

As she drew close to the house, an amazing event occurred. Wendy, a firm believer in angels, saw the biggest angel anyone could ever imagine towering over the house. It was a behemoth of angels and Wendy described it as being as tall as the Eiffel Tower! She knew at once in her heart that this was her mother's angel and that the end would be very soon.

The following afternoon, when Wendy was sitting by her mother's bedside and holding her hand, Wendy's mother slipped from this world into the next. Feelings of love filled the room and even through the grief of parting, Wendy felt peace descend. She knew the huge angel was now taking her mother's hand and leading her into the next life. It is a vision that will stay with Wendy for ever.

Deep peace, pure grey of the dew to you,

Deep peace, pure blue of the sky to you,

Deep peace of the running wave to you,

Deep peace of the flowing air to you,

Deep peace of the quiet earth to you . . .

Celtic Blessing

EXERCISE:
Writing a Way through Grief and Loss

For the newly bereaved or those who have experienced a profound loss such as the irretrievable breakdown of a relationship or a divorce, starting a spiritual diary can be a wonderful way to express thoughts and feelings that might otherwise be difficult to articulate. For so many people talking at such a time is particularly difficult and they find themselves alone in their thoughts.

If you are grieving or mourning a loss of some sort, keeping a special diary in your Angel Journal will focus your attention on the deepest sensations and illuminate what might be done to alleviate the most painful. It may prove to be a difficult exercise to begin with, but as time passes it will be revealing and may be of great comfort to you.

As we have explained before, if you look for the smallest signs that the angels are close and record these in your journal you will discover just how often they do leave signs in your life. We cannot emphasise enough that the more we recognise these signs, the more frequently they will appear. You may have to start with simply noting down a blessing, the smallest blessing in perhaps a very depressing day, such as a slight glimmer of sunshine in a grey sky. Concentrate on this little gift and you will have found the positive ray of light in the dark. By appreciating even the smallest of blessings, the following day more will be apparent.

Journal keeping is to be recommended no matter what your circumstances. You do not have to be suffering because of loss. Whether you are coping with illness or having problems at work, worrying about elderly parents or worrying about children – whatever your problem – writing about it will help. Keeping a diary of your feelings may be the beginning of the change you wish would occur in your life. By recording in black and white the very things that you feel are holding you back you will see more clearly how to alter the situation. Should you feel fear, your fear will be brought under control a little by the very act of giving it space in your diary, as often writing down what exactly we fear or are worrying about will clarify the situation for us.

Metamorphosis

If we learn to read accurately the signs around us in nature, who knows what adventures will follow? We do not have to be super-sensitive types to interpret them and act on them. Marianne Lensink, for one, could be described as a very down-to-earth Dutch lady. Extraordinary things, however, happened in Marianne's life, turning her unexpectedly into an author:

Marianne had been happily married for many years to Hans, with whom she enjoyed a particularly close relationship. This made the pain even more acute when Hans died from a brain tumour. It was at this point in her life that Marianne started to write a diary in the manner suggested on page 191. Always a wonderful way of getting feelings out, keeping a diary helps make sense of the grieving process. Little could Marianne have known, however, that over the next two years her diary would be filled with amazing spiritual experiences. Marianne came to believe firmly that Hans's spirit was steering these wonderful events.

The day after Hans's funeral, Marianne and her daughters went to visit his grave. They wanted to look at the wonderful flowers that people had sent and to be able to fully appreciate them in peace now that the service was over. It was raining heavily when they set out but as soon as they arrived at the grave the sun appeared.

Mesmerised, they stood and watched with awe as from the midst of the flowers a cloud of yellow butterflies emerged!

One of Marianne's daughters observed that it was a sign from her daddy. It was only later that Marianne became aware of how significant was the symbolism of the butterflies. When she was reading some time later about how butterflies have been regarded as a symbol of the soul for generations, Marianne was moved to tears. The metamorphosis of the butterfly symbolised the soul regenerating in the afterlife.

Five weeks after the death of Hans, Marianne and one of her daughters decided to take a trip to Greece, which was one of Hans's favourite countries. Marianne hoped that she might find a little peace there and indeed a little sleep, both of which had been eluding her. At last, sleep came and Marianne found herself sleeping for twelve hours at a stretch. For seven nights, this sleep refreshed and restored Marianne, physically at least. Then, on the last morning before she was due to go home, something extraordinary happened. Glancing towards the other side of the bed, Marianne saw Hans lying next to her! He was clear and solid, and Marianne emphasises that she was awake; this was no dream and it was certainly not the product of her imagination. After her return from Greece, Hans was to appear to Marianne several more times, giving her such a strong feeling of continuity and love.

Eventually, Marianne found herself giving talks and interviews, explaining the wonderful events in her life and giving comfort and hope to other bereaved people. Stories of similar experiences flooded in and it became obvious that there was a book for her to write. Marianne's book *Guided Coincidences* followed, offering insight, comfort and hope to its many readers.

What lies behind us and what lies before us are tiny matters compared to what lies within us.

Ralph Waldo Emerson
American essayist and poet (1803–1882)

*Your true essence is your soul, which is eternal
and exists in an ocean of love.*

You are not your body.

Brian L. Weiss M.D.
Psychotherapist and researcher

❧ *Angel Top Tip* ❧

At the beginning of each week, write down in
your Angel Journal your goals for the coming
days, your aspirations and the positive
qualities you want to welcome into your life.
In time, these weekly forecasts will become a
self-fulfilling prophecy, with the positive
written words preceding your positive actions.

Let Nature Signpost Your Way
to Inner Peace

Very few of us are lucky enough to be rewarded with the sight
of a huge angel as Wendy was, or a whole flock of butterflies
as Marianne was, albeit both in distressing circumstances.
However, as we have already seen when discussing the
messages that the angels send us through signs and symbols,
we can take great comfort in the natural world around us.
Nature can soothe, heal and rest the soul; if we can appreciate
the beauty and indeed the usefulness of nature, we will be on
our way to finding peace.

The Native North American peoples knew only too well the

importance of nature, including how their own lives depended on it. Outside their tepees they would hang what has become known in the West as a mandala (the same word is also used to describe the intricate motifs used in Buddhist and Hindu art to symbolise the Universe). This would be fashioned out of fine twigs or sticks into a traditional circular shape. Threads would be woven across the circle and on these they would hang symbols representative of their lives, such as a swathe of buffalo hair, bird's feathers, plants or small stone arrows – all the things that nature provided for them. Each morning, on leaving their tepee the first thing they would see would be this mandala, reminding them of the importance of the natural world around them and a token of silent thanks for this bounty.

Imagine your own mandala: what symbols of nature, vital to your life, would be hung there? Decorate your mandala in your mind's eye and feel the peace and tranquillity this mental picture provokes. (Use it to inspire you in the exercise below.)

There are moments in all our lives when the heart is filled with peace. The face of a sleeping baby, a wonderful sunset, the sight of daffodils blooming in spring or rainbows after a storm can all soothe the soul, offering glimpses of the divine. The crunch of fallen autumn leaves under foot, the lapping of the sea and the patter of gentle rain encourage the heart to sigh with deep peace. Trees are often referred to as 'open air cathedrals' as they command such sacred feelings. Mountains, waterfalls and forests are regarded the world over as sacred places.

Nature can brighten the spiritual light inside us all if we let it. Writing in twelfth-century Europe, Bernard of Clairvaux said he found 'heaven' in the book of nature. He saw nature as an allegory of heavenly things. 'I have no other masters than the Beech and the Oak,' he wrote. From the philosophy of the North American Natives to the teachings of Zen to medieval scripture, nature breathes harmony and peace into each life.

EXERCISE:
Create Your Own Seasonal Peace Altar

In previous books, we have explained how to create a 'home altar'. A simple home altar works on the same principles as the mandala we described above.

* Choose a small tile, woven mat or piece of flat wood and place on it objects important and relevant to your life. These can be items from nature, pebbles or shells that remind you of a wonderful holiday, pine cones or flowers. You can even include photographs or whatever else feels close to you.

* Place a candle in the centre. For a few moments each week light the candle (making sure that you will not leave it unattended and that it can't accidentally set light to anything!). Then sit and meditate on the bounties of nature and the peace and blessings that are yours.

* As the seasons pass, you could change this home altar and add flowers that are in season, berries, leaves or winter twigs. It will be well worth the effort to have this lovely display and to take a few moments to create inner peace.

*Few are altogether deaf to the preaching of pine
trees. Their sermons on the mountains go to our
hearts and if people in general can be gotten to
the woods even for once to hear the trees speak
for themselves, all difficulties in the way of
forest preservation would vanish.*

John Muir
Preservationist (1803–1882)

❧ *Angel Top Tip* ❧

Find a photograph of yourself taken on an
occasion when you were happy and smiling.
Place it on your bedroom mirror or behind the
front door, then make sure you look at it
before you leave the house each day. It will
remind you of those happy times and confirm
that they will be with you once more. So start
the day with a happy image.

Replacing Negative Patterns

It's all very well saying that we should look for the signs in nature and make a concerted effort to find inner peace, but is it possible that we might sometimes be sabotaging our own peace of mind without even realising it?

As we saw in the Star of Self-Belief, we all learned patterns of behaviour and defence mechanisms as very young children. These may no longer be necessary in our lives, but subconsciously we still adhere to them. We may have acquired negative thoughts about certain situations or people that are now holding us back.

To complicate the situation further, we may be influenced by other factors in addition to our personal conditioning. The famous Austrian psychologist Carl Jung wrote a great deal about something called the 'collective unconscious'. This term refers to those elements of an individual's unconscious mind that are derived from the experiences of society as a whole. Could we be picking up signals and attitudes from others without realising it? Could these signals and attitudes be influencing our own outlook and peace of mind? If we take a quiet moment to try to picture events and people in our early lives, we may unearth the roots of a pattern that we can begin to release, and also realise how we are influenced by society as a whole.

Start to pay attention to the patterns of thinking that influence your day. When a negative thought enters your mind, replace it at once with a more positive one. Tell yourself that you will not allow the past to hold you back. You *can* have a peaceful life and you *will* have a peaceful life. Where possible, simply avoid those people who affect you in a negative way; don't feel guilty about it as your peace of mind is at stake here. Wish them well, forgive any hurt and then move on. You are replacing the old patterns with new and it is not always as difficult as you might think. However, if you do find that you need support, don't be ashamed to draw on the guidance of a professional counsellor. Be persistent, positive and determined that peace of mind shall be yours.

The stillness and the peace of NOW

enfold you in perfect gentleness.

Little Book of Miracles

Divine Star

As you begin to observe your thoughts more and more, you may notice how they change from one moment to the next. Can you witness the battle going on within yourself? Consider what steps you might take to bring that battle to an end.

MEDITATION:
On the Gifts of Peace

Now that you have worked hard on welcoming the Stars of Self-Belief, Gratitude, Harmony, Trust and Courage into your life, you are ready to receive the gifts of all your efforts. Let this meditation reward you with peace.

* As you close your eyes, take a long, deep breath . . . Take another deep breath, and feel how safe and loved you are. Breathe in the stillness and the silence.

* Feel the strength in yourself, the clarity that is yours.

Notice how all the energy in your body is golden light, flowing freely through every part of you. Recognise how light you feel, how empowered you are. See the light that is radiating from within you as it sends out rays of light all around you.

* Feel the peace within you, the peace that lives in every cell of your being. You are ready now to say: 'I have peace.' Notice how effortlessly you are able to bring peace into your heart. As you say these words, the energetic beauty of dancing stars flows through you.

* Breathing in the stillness, it is now time to say: 'I love myself. I let go with peace and love. I forgive myself.'

* Wake up from living in fear, self-doubt and the lack of faith that is rooted in the past and that dwells in the collective psyche of all mankind. Put all negative thoughts out of your mind. Declare your freedom. Declare your oneness with love and harmony and peace.

* As you surface from your meditative state, make a resolution to carry peace in your heart always. Joyfully accept your divine guidance. You will be open to new ideas, new thoughts, new hopes and aspirations. Everything that so recently seemed a problem no longer exists. Allow peace and joy to vibrate in every part of your life.

✎ *Angel Top Tip* ✎

Choose a positive affirmation from this book
and remind yourself of it daily. You could even
write it down and put it where you will see it
each morning, such as stuck to your bathroom
mirror, to help start your day in the manner in
which you would like it to continue.

Touched by an Angel

It can be hard to find inner peace when we are wracked by
doubts and fears about our choices in life. Life-changing
decisions cause many of us sleepless nights and anxious days,
and some decisions in life are harder to make than others.
This was certainly the case for Ruth:

Since leaving university ten years previously, she had always
lived in shared accommodation with friends. Although this
had been for the most part a happy experience for her, at the
age of thirty-one Ruth decided a measure of independence
was called for. Enjoying a well paid job and having a solid
circle of friends, she decided that she would buy a house she
had seen for sale locally. Her offer was accepted and now here
she was, sitting alone in her little kitchen on her very first
night in her new home.

It would be fair to say that Ruth was filled with trepidation
as she stared at her bank statement, which lay open on the
kitchen table. In her heart she knew everything would be fine
but she found herself shaking at the very thought of being a
householder and all the responsibilities that this entailed.

Contemplating her future, she felt her spirits fall. She felt very alone and close to tears.

Suddenly, she sensed a gentle stroking on her head and a tingling sensation ran down her spine. Instinctively she turned around but there was of course no one there. She wasn't afraid at all; in fact quite the reverse, she felt a warm, happy glow fill her and lift her flagging spirits.

A short time later, she went to see a friend whose aunt was also visiting. She was fascinated when the aunt announced that she was a medium. 'And I have a message for you,' the woman said. 'Your angel wants you to know that she is close and watching over you; she has made contact but you didn't recognise her.' Ruth at once understood: the touch had been that of her angel!

The concept of angels had never entered Ruth's head before, but she instinctively understood that at her lowest moment that night in the kitchen she had been open, vulnerable and in need of comfort and peace of mind. The sensations of peace have stayed with Ruth since that night. She is eternally grateful for the medium's message, for her angel's visit and for the feelings of confidence and peace that have since grown within her.

AFFIRMATION

Today, I experience the peace that surpasses all understanding. I am willing to release any fear or negative thoughts.

EXERCISE:
Angel Dreams

We all need healing in our lives. We may have physical problems, emotional concerns or simply lack self-belief. Whatever our problem, the angels can help, and a good time to approach them is just before we go to sleep each night.

* If you wish to welcome some angelic healing into your life, simply close your eyes and relax. Let the day's events slip away from your mind; make room for the angels to come in and give you healing and love. Whatever your problem, the angels will never judge you as they love you unconditionally.

* Feel the peace enter your heart as you allow these magical beings to enter it. They love you simply for being you. Focus on what you would like to share and ask your guides. Feel the comfort and love they give, secure in the knowledge that your angels will always be by your side.

* Ask for peace to calm you in the coming day and peace to allow you to accept the many blessings that that day will bring. Ask for healing in whatever respect you need it most.

* Just before you slip into sleep, tell yourself that your angel is listening and peace is yours for the asking.

Let Peace be Yours

Many individuals have the mistaken notion that peace must be attained on an external, even global level before their lives can be harmonious, but this is not so. If we focus on peace individually, we can find it within ourselves.

However, we must first adopt the mental attitude that

peace is already ours and act as though this were true, by focusing on what we wish to experience. We must create a sacred space of serenity within our own hearts through the continual, conscious, creative and simple choice to live, breathe and be Peace in our thoughts, words and deeds. No matter how many times our negative thought patterns return, we can dismiss them by knowing that they no longer have any power over us.

Maintaining a peaceful balance in everyday life requires inner peace, self-awareness and the willingness to live consciously in our hearts from moment to moment. Peace and inspiration are gifts to give and receive throughout our lives. Our lives are all equally valuable and every second in them matters because our stories, our choices and our kindnesses touch the lives of so many people besides our own.

Divine Star

Do you know where your compassion for another begins and ends? Let your compassion flow freely, for once it begins in you it will spread to the world.

EXERCISE:
Align Yourself with Peace

Pure peace manifests itself through acts of kindness and love. In this exercise you will begin to align your peaceful thoughts and energy with a major goal or desire you wish to realise.

Step 1

Determine your goal or goals:

_____

_____

Step 2

Make a list of your beliefs regarding this goal or goals. For instance, what practical steps might a person need to take to achieve it? And how would achieving it make you feel? Could your goal be defined as an act of kindness or love?

_____

_____

Step 3

In what ways would achieving your goal enhance your sense of inner peace and the peace of those around you?

_____

_____

Step 4

Go for it!

> ### ❧ *Angel Top Tip* ❧
>
> In your Angel Journal, write a wish list of
> seven requests for help and guidance from the
> angels, cosmos, Universe or whatever you wish
> to call the higher power that oversees all our
> lives. Go back to it in seven weeks' time and
> re-read it. Has anything changed?

Peace Forever

Peace begins with us individually and radiates out from our hearts to our friends, families and colleagues. Once we are at peace with ourselves, we can begin to lay the foundations for peace in the world.

But inner peace may seem elusive when we doubt ourselves or are troubled by anxiety, fear or grief. However, it is always ours for the asking once we become aware of the angelic presence in our lives.

The angels communicate with us in so many different ways, which can range from small, seemingly insignificant experiences to dramatic moments of spiritual synchronicity. Our dreams may contain messages from our angels and even sudden flashes of inspiration may indicate an angelic presence, once we know to look for them.

The angels are there for us all, including you; simply believe the signs and say thank you. They will bring you peace.

**STAR POINTS TO
PONDER:**

I make time for relaxation.

*I will de-clutter my mind, workplace
and home.*

I look for messages from the angels.

*I set aside a period each week to
meditate.*

I stop to smell the flowers.

*I ask my angel to bring peace into my
heart.*

*I am at peace and take peace with me
wherever I go.*

7

The Star of Love

*Send out love and harmony, put your mind
and body in a peaceful place and then allow
the Universe to work in the perfect way that it
knows how.*

Dr Wayne W. Dyer
Psychotherapist, lecturer and author

The Essence of Life

The Star of Love represents what is probably the most important element in life itself.

We can have wealth, beauty, leisure and riches beyond measure, but if we are without love we have little of true value. In a recent interview, a famous pop star bemoaned the fact that he had never found true love. He explained that although fame and fortune were his in abundance, he would be willing to trade it all in for a stable relationship and a loving family – a very telling revelation.

Like that celebrity, we all need love but so many of us seem to spend our lives searching fruitlessly for it. However, perhaps we are looking in the wrong place to begin with. We must first learn to love ourselves in order to be ready to receive love. For if we don't love ourselves, or believe ourselves worthy of love, how can we expect others to be drawn to us? Loving ourselves isn't about being self-centred or arrogant, but about accepting ourselves as we are, warts and all. Once we have come to terms with ourselves as we are, we can begin to move on. Learning to love ourselves isn't always easy, but it is a crucial first step in attracting love into our lives.

And even if we do have lingering doubts about our own worthiness to receive love, the angels have none. While we may sometimes feel profoundly let down by the love of others, the angels will never disappoint us. Their love is constant and unconditional. We are literally never alone. At times of crisis or great emotional upheaval, we can always take our problems to the angels. Should we encounter a problem we feel we could not possibly discuss with others, no matter how close, we can always confide in the heavenly powers. If we communicate with them through meditation, prayer and affirmations, we have only to ask and help will be at hand.

So ask the angels to reveal the power of love in your life and recognise their help when it is offered. Once more the most important ingredient in this form of communication is to believe. Then, without doubt, you will receive.

Love is not learned, because there never was a
time in which you knew it not.

A Course in Miracles

MEDITATION:
The Star of Love

In this meditation, you will be connecting with your angelic
guides and discovering how to bring love into whatever
seems to be the most challenging situation for you.

* As you close your eyes, take a deep breath. Feel your
  body relaxing, releasing. Inhale and exhale deeply, slowly, moving into a space of complete relaxation, into that
  safe space within. In your mind's eye, surround yourself
  with a ring of pure white light. This light protects you
  and you will always be safe within it.

* Bring into your awareness a situation that is troubling
  you, one that deeply saddens you or one that you may
  feel responsibility for. On the other side of your ring of
  light, allow an image to form in your mind that sums up
  the situation. Allow all the negative energy you personally feel around the situation to show up as well in whatever form it chooses. Knowing you are completely safe
  and empowered, invite any other form of negative energy that has been created by this situation to also show
  up.

* See yourself staring down into the ground and willing all
  the roots of the negativity to come up and out. In your
  mind's eye, send them to hover with the rest of the negative energy associated with the situation. When you feel
  the situation is fully represented, will the negativity to
  explode. Notice that the combination of the explosion
  and your desire to be done with the negativity has
  caused all that was negative to transform into millions of
  stars and a billion tiny rays of light that twinkle far away
  in the distance.

* Continue exploding the negativity until all you can see
  in front of you is the cluster of stars and the streaks of

light. Tell the Universe that this beauty is what you intend.

* Ask your angels and the Universe for guidance in helping you see clearly what steps are needed to transform this situation. Reflect on this for a little while. Then ask for the resolve to see these steps through.

* Slowly and gently return to everyday consciousness. As you surface, bring back with you the steps and the resolve. As you move out of your meditation, feel the courage pulsing in your body and know that you are the creator of Love, and that you *are* love . . .

AFFIRMATION

I am love, and I am loved.

Believing and Receiving Love

There is something inside each and every one of us that always is looking for the answers in life. We may want to know why we are here, what life is all about and what lies beyond this planet that we call home. However, while many of the answers to the mysteries of life may elude us, we can make a great deal of sense of our world purely through the medium of love. Love is the fundamental absolute truth of life. It is all there is and all that we truly seek. It's ours right now and always has been there for us to activate in our lives. Gentle yet all-powerful, love defines us at our best.

When we choose to love ourselves, we're affirming our own greatness. We're saying to the Universe: 'I am lovable. I deserve happiness. I deserve success.' We're giving permission to others and to the magical workings of the Universe to love us back. If we choose to love ourselves, the Universe will mirror this back to us. And we can *decide* to love ourselves; it's a choice – a simple, yet extremely profound choice that can have miraculous ramifications.

If you want to bring more love into your own life, you can begin simply with the intention to love yourself. Say to yourself right now: 'I love myself!'

Now, how do you feel when you say or think those three little words? Perhaps at first you feel uncomfortable and a little bit embarrassed. But stay with it and repeat the words again and again. Can you sense the subtle shift in energy that takes place each time you say or think them?

As you repeat, 'I love myself', the colour of your energy actually changes. It becomes brighter, more vibrant. You will begin to radiate with the light you've seen in others, the same light you've been attracted to in other people. And you will begin to realise just why you're so mesmerised by certain people.

It's all about self-love, and although you've had the ability to love yourself all along, you may have needed to remind yourself of it. So say again and again, 'I love myself', and watch as your world shifts. Then continue to say it all the time, especially when you least feel like saying it, when you feel like it's simply not true or you don't deserve to be loved by anyone. By saying it at precisely those moments, you open yourself up to the possibility of its being true. Then, the impossible becomes possible, what was complicated becomes simple, and confusion disintegrates to be replaced by great clarity.

It doesn't need to be difficult to love ourselves. That's the beauty of it. Why shouldn't it be easy? Each and every one of us deserves love. All it takes is our intention. It's a decision and we all make hundreds of decisions every day. This one, the decision simply to say 'I love myself', will change your life. Repeating this simple affirmation on a daily basis will help you let go of any emotional baggage and wash away what was never yours to begin with; it will open up spaces in your heart, making room for happiness and success.

But if you feel hesitant about saying you love yourself, the chances are you're contemplating a mental list of all the reasons you supposedly don't deserve love.

It is surprising how many people believe they don't deserve love. Life may have dealt them some pretty severe blows and they might have found themselves flat on the floor with no apparent means of getting up. A chance remark or even a joke at an inopportune moment can sometimes fester and grow out of all proportion in our psyches until we believe we are unattractive and therefore unworthy of love. Similarly, exam failure can result in depression, in which instance, making the effort to try again can seem like an alien concept. If we grew up in an environment that was not particularly nurturing, we may somehow see this as our fault, believing that we were not shown love and affection because we did not deserve it.

If this strikes a chord with you, then it's time to release all those internalised voices that come up with excuses as to why you shouldn't love yourself. Let the voices and the excuses go; to devote energy to them is to waste energy. Learn how to receive love in your life, first by giving yourself permission to love yourself. Make a conscious decision now to be the kind of person who radiates light, walking through life with an unshakeable inner joy and confidence.

That said, however great your resolve, there can be times when you might feel stuck in an emotional rut that it is very difficult to get out of. At these times, the unspoken questions facing you are, 'Do I want to stay in this place? Do I want to remain unhappy?' Unless being unhappy serves you in some way, the answer is, of course, 'No.'

As we know, life is short and the Universe is patiently waiting to give us what we most desire. The Universe will gladly support us in getting out of any rut we're in. If we realise this, the question then becomes, 'How do I do it?' And the answer is simple: 'Open yourself to love.' That's all it takes.

When we give ourselves the permission to love, we give ourselves the permission to be happy.

We can open ourselves to love by loving ourselves, by beginning to notice love in all of its forms, and by being willing to give and receive love. If this seems impossible at first, then begin with the healing influence of angelic love. Know that you are loved unconditionally by the angels and the Universe, and that if they believe you deserve to be loved, then you do. It's as simple as that.

> *Love yourself enough to take a break.*

Edward England
Writer

AFFIRMATION

I love myself.

❧ *Angel Top Tip* ❧

Now you know that you are love, and loved,
go and spread it around.

EXERCISE:
Sowing the Seeds of Love

There are many ways in which you can encourage love to grow in your life. This exercise is designed to help you focus on the seeds of love that are already present in your life, waiting to be nurtured through your positive thinking.

Step 1 I love to . . .

> In your Angel Journal or on the lines below, write down several activities that you love. Think of things that are absolutely easy for you to do – things that you may not have received any training in, but are just good at.

_____

_____

Step 2 I am . . .

> Write down a few top qualities that you love about yourself or that others have seen in you. What are your talents and strengths?

_____

_____

_____

Step 3 Take responsibility

> If you feel that you don't have enough of something in your life, make a list. What do you lack and why? And what steps could you take to fill that lack?

Step 4 Think love . . .

Fill in the following gaps here or in your journal to create sentences that reflect the good you already create in your life and also what you want to create in your life.

I create _____ for myself.

I create _____ for myself.

I create _____ for myself.

I create _____ for myself.

I create _____ for myself.

How loving and peaceful is a life that we create from a place of awareness! Take the time each day to list mentally your creations in life and become aware of your divine potential in all that you do and in all your relationships.

You can never repay all you have been given by the Creator, accept the gifts. Live and share them.

Anne Wilson Schaef
Writer and lecturer

Love and Relationships

Most of us associate love with relationships, but what exactly is a relationship? We may think of relationships as our dealings with those close to us or the people with whom we have to spend time each day. The truth is that we're in relationship with every other being on this planet; we are all related and are truly one. When we allow ourselves to love other people, we are extending the gift of grace. Or, to put it another way, love is there when we surrender into love.

Love defines who we are. We can always be open to love or decide to push love away, by deciding who is or who is not worthy of our love. However, absolute love knows no boundaries or restrictions.

Every single one of us is loved by the Universe and in turn each one of us has been granted some special gift, some special interest or some special way of impacting on this world, so that it becomes a better place for everyone. You too have the potential to live at the level of Gandhi or Mother Teresa. The question you must first ask yourself is: 'Am I willing to define, embrace and trust my divine purpose persistently and patiently?' Let the answer be 'yes', then see what practical steps you can take right here, right now.

Love conquers all things:
let us too give in to love.

Virgil
Poet (70–19 BC)

❧ *Angel Top Tip* ❧

Many people believe that they have a
personal guardian angel, who looks after them
and helps them reach their true potential. To
discover yours, sit quietly, contemplate your
current position in life and which direction you
wish it to take. Ask your angel for her name, and
it may pop into your head immediately. Write it
down and know that this is your special angel.
You will be able to call on her whenever you
need extra help and guidance. Also call on her
when you want to know how best to fulfil your
true potential and live a productive life,
helping others.

EXERCISE:
Become a Volunteer

Somebody out there needs you. You might not know who
just yet, but you can make a difference to someone's life just
by sparing a little of your time and kindness.

You will need:
    Self-belief (a measure of)
    Dedication
    A pinch of bravery

* Every community needs volunteers like you. What do
  you care about? Who do you want to help? The possibilities are endless: you can become a hospital visitor or

befriend someone who is confined to their own home. You can become a local youth worker or help out at a retirement home. You can get out and about in the fresh air by taking part in your local conservation projects, or become involved in animal sanctuaries.

* Take a look in your telephone directory to see which organisations listed there appeal to you. Or visit your library to find out more about ways you can become involved in your local community. Share a little of the love that you have to spare with those who really need it.

> *The whole world can love you, but that love will not make you happy.*
>
> *What will make you happy is to share all the love you have inside you.*
>
> *That is the love that will make a difference.*
>
> **Don Miguel Ruiz**
> Toltec shaman and author

Little Tokens of Love

The evidence suggests that the more we are willing to reach out lovingly to others, the more love we will receive in return. Several years ago, a television programme tried to find out why some people in particular elicit a positive response from others. Researchers sent two women out onto the street with instructions to ask people at random for help. They were told to ask for change for a five pound note and also to ask for directions. One woman received a clear and positive response from those she approached, while the other lady was literally cold-shouldered. Why was this so? It appears that the first woman was told to touch the person she asked for help and to smile broadly, while the second woman was instructed to do neither. A friendly tap on the arm and a warm smile nurtured a sense of trust and instant cooperation in others, as people responded to the woman's warmth and the feeling of being liked.

Giving love to others can be a very subtle process. For instance, we might offer to help someone in a small task, and our simple deed of kindness will promote feelings of kindness in return. A friend once told us that when she saw someone who looked sad or lonely when she was walking along the street, she would throw an invisible blanket of love over them as she passed! It's a lovely concept and even if the person on the receiving end didn't see the blanket, we're sure the angels did.

> There is a light that shines beyond all things on Earth,
>
> Beyond us all, beyond the heavens, beyond the highest, the very highest heavens.
>
> This is the light that shines in our hearts.
>
> **Chandogya Upanishad**

Divine Star

Now, here is the thing! The more affection,
kindness and loving thoughts we give out, the
more we will receive. Just like a bank account,
the more we deposit into the vaults of love, the
greater will be the interest returned, and the
more we love others, the more we will realise just
what deserving people we are ourselves.

Love is patient, love is kind and envies no one.

Love is never boastful, nor conceited, nor rude;
never selfish nor quick to take offence.

Love keeps no score of wrongs; does not gloat
over other men's sins, but delights in the
truth.

There is nothing love cannot face.

There is no limit to its faith, its hope and its
endurance;

Love will never come to an end.

I Corinthians 13:4–8

Today, I am a unique expression of Divine love.

Angel Hugs

It's clear that we can bring love into the world through so many different means. The smallest of gestures such as a kiss or a hug can sometimes be the most powerful. Instinctively when we see someone in distress, we put our arms around them in a gesture of comfort and solidarity. When we are children and scrape our knees in the playground, or are upset for any reason, a kiss and a hug from a parent will make everything so much better. We kiss and hug in happy times too, such as when we receive good news and have cause for celebration. Such little gestures of human contact are truly precious.

However, not everyone is fortunate enough to have someone close to whom they can reach out in times of happiness or sadness:

This was the situation in which Enid found herself. She had lived alone for many years, her parents and siblings long deceased. Not having married or had children of her own, she often found herself feeling terribly lonely. Attending her local church brought some comfort to her and in truth her friends from church were always willing to visit her and keep her company. Their companionship was, though, she told us, 'never quite the same as belonging to someone'.

Enid's feelings of loneliness came to a head one morning, when she woke in a great deal of pain. Suffering from arthritis, she found some days much more painful than others, but today was the worst in terms of pain that she could ever recall. It took her a long time to get herself dressed and descend the stairs to her little kitchen to make a cup of tea. The effort was exhausting and she finally sank into her armchair, close to tears. Adding to her distress was the fact that the following day would be her eighty-fifth birthday and she had no one to celebrate it with.

The day wore on and though the pain improved somewhat with her medication, Enid's mood didn't lift. With a heavy heart she climbed slowly back to bed that night. There, she prayed, asking God if he had a spare angel and, if He did, would the angel help Enid to count her blessings and feel brighter on her birthday?

Enid's birthday dawned and to her delight her arthritis was nowhere near as painful this morning as she rose from her bed. Reaching the kitchen, she started to feel a little cheerier. Suddenly there was the noise of her letterbox opening and to her surprise a good few cards dropped onto the mat. Several of her friends had remembered her and instead of the one or two cards that she usually received, this time at least eight envelopes met her gaze.

Opening her cards and placing them on her mantelpiece she thought again about her prayer the night before. She said out loud, 'God, thank you. The angels have been working on my behalf!'

At that precise moment it happened: Enid had the sensation of arms encircling her and a warm glow surrounding her. She had a feeling of pure love enveloping her. As the tears flowed down her cheeks from sheer happiness, she thought of what a wonderful blessing she had to add to her list that birthday. How could she ever feel alone and unloved again, with the knowledge that the angels had given her a heavenly hug?

Love is the energy from which all people and things are made.

You are connected to everything in your world through love.

Brian L. Weiss M.D.
Psychotherapist and researcher

AFFIRMATION

Today, I am free of all problems, all fear and all possibilities of failure. I fill myself with love and abundance.

❧ *Angel Top Tip* ☙

We don't have to make grand gestures in order to bring love into the world. A simple act of kindness, such as a smile, a word of praise, a gesture of appreciation, remembering to send a birthday card or joining in a celebration such as a party can mean everything to someone else.

Love in Black and White

Family celebrations such as weddings, christenings and birthdays are often occasions on which we can make our love for each other clear. They can become events that stay with us for ever. In our next story, Marjorie remembers when a birthday party became charged with special significance:

'It was exactly twenty-five years ago today,' Marjorie recalled, 'when we had that lovely picnic for my father.' Senior members of the family remembered it well, and they began to talk about the day as they sat down to Sunday lunch in Marjorie's dining room.

Tom, Marjorie's father, had been celebrating his seventieth birthday on a glorious summer's day. The whole family had driven to the coast for a picnic, where they had enjoyed an afternoon full of fun and laughter. Tom's grandchildren were very young but joined in the celebrations too, devouring the huge cake their parents had taken along with them to cut ceremoniously after lunch. It had been a very special occasion, especially so as Tom had sadly died a week later.

And so here they were now, gathered together on her father's birthday once more, all these years later. 'The only thing I regret about that day was losing my camera,' said Marjorie. 'I don't even recall taking any photographs,' she continued. 'I simply forgot and then managed to lose it!' Throughout the intervening years, the loss of the camera had been a source of regret for the family because no one had a record of that last, special birthday. 'We have all the memories in our heads,' Marjorie said, 'but I really wish we had a photograph of him at the party – we have so very few of him.'

The afternoon drew on and they found themselves talking more and more about Tom and his special birthday. By the time most of the extended family had left, everyone was feeling quite sad. 'Cheer up,' said Marjorie's husband. 'Nothing you can do about it now!'

A couple of weeks later, Marjorie decided to have a thorough clean of their spare bedroom, intending to give away a lot of bits and bobs to the summer fair organised by their local church. The idea had been on her mind for a while but the urge became compelling and she felt very keen to get started on the task. Chests of drawers and old cupboards not searched through for ages were all cleared out and lots of hidden treasures came to light.

Right at the top of the old wardrobe was a box containing photographs and a dusty old camera. 'Goodness knows how long this has been here,' Marjorie said.

Her husband remarked that the camera clearly had film inside and for fun he would take it along to the local shop to see if it might be developed. 'Little hope,' he said, 'but worth a try out of curiosity.' When he handed in the film, he noticed that it was an old black and white reel. The man in the shop said the film was so old he doubted it would print, but he would be happy to try.

Days later Marjorie went to see if the film had been successfully printed and was delighted to find that, to everyone's surprise, it had printed quite well. Leaving the shop, she walked to the car park and, sitting in her car, opened the packet of photographs. At this point, Marjorie almost dropped them with shock, for smiling up at her was her father, cutting his seventieth birthday cake at the picnic! Tears of happiness rolled down her cheeks and she could not wait to get home to show her family the precious pictures.

Several wonderful photographs of that special day had been printed, clear and sharp. However, Marjorie says that she can't recall taking any of them. On seeing them, Marjorie's daughter said, 'Mum, I reckon the angels took these for you.'

'Well,' Marjorie replied, 'that might be the case. They certainly pointed me in the right direction to find them, that's for sure!'

Where love abounds,
the angels hover overhead.

Anon

Divine Star

Angel messages can be timely reminders of the
love in our lives. Those messages may take
many unexpected and subtle forms, but when
we are really in need of them they will often
be very clear to us.

Vera's angels are real

Like Marjorie's story, our next tale involves loss and an
unexpected sign of the angels' presence:

All her life Vera had attended church. She had a strong faith
and believed firmly in the angels, whom she loved. She had
been a keen member of the same church for many years and
was involved in many of its activities, especially the Mothers'
Union.

Life had not been without its problems and tears from time
to time for Vera, but a loving husband and children had
brought her much happiness. Widowed for many years now,
Vera was in her late eighties and struggling with her health.
Although she had enjoyed a full and interesting life, she nevertheless clung tenaciously to this world, as so many of us do
when the end is near. But when she was finally admitted to
hospital, it became clear to her family that she wouldn't be

with them for much longer. Her son Stephen and his wife Barbara had the lovely idea of bringing the little angel plaque Vera kept by her bedside at home to the hospital, where they laid it on Vera's pillow for comfort.

One evening, Stephen, Barbara, Vera's daughter Margaret and other family members were sitting around Vera's bed, holding her hand and comforting her. She was clearly on the brink of death but still would not let herself go. Eventually, Stephen told the family to go home and get some rest. They had all been by the bedside a long time and tiredness was setting in. They agreed and left.

Now Vera's breathing was heavy and laboured; she was clearly fighting the inevitable. Stephen gently held his mother's hand and told her it was all right to let go – not to be afraid, everything would be fine. Taking the little angel plaque from the pillow beside Vera's head, he placed it firmly in her hand and curled her fingers around it with the obvious message that her angels were waiting for her. At once Vera's breathing became calm and shallow; then, within moments, she slipped away into the next world. It was all so peaceful and fitting for a lady holding such faith.

Stephen sat quietly, taking it all in with mixed emotions. He felt very sad that his mother had gone, but was also relieved that at last her struggle was over and that she had been so peaceful at the very end. After a few moments, Stephen rose to find the medical staff and inform them of events. He gazed wistfully at his mother, her hand holding the little angel plaque tightly, then turned and walked towards the door. As he reaching for the door handle, he looked back into the room, where suddenly he saw something he found difficult to comprehend.

The angel plaque slowly left his mother's hand, slid across the bedclothes and onto the floor, where it broke into two pieces. It was, he thought, impossible; even had his mother's hand released the angel plaque, it would have simply stayed on the bed next to her. The bedclothes had not been pulled taut and it appeared impossible that this object could have moved so far across the wide bed by itself. Instead, it was as if an unseen force had propelled the plaque to the floor! At this point we should tell readers that Stephen had been a policeman for all his working life, and was a down-to-earth, practical man – the very last person to be fanciful in any way. To quote him: 'I thought I had seen everything, but this was amazing.'

Relating this incident to his family, he was greeted with looks of amazement. His sister Margaret, however, also believed in angels and she saw this as some kind of a sign, although at that moment she was unsure as to what exactly that might be. The following day, the family gathered at Vera's little bungalow, arriving all at the same time. Walking into the lounge, they once more were met with a sight that made them stare in amazement. Vera had always had a crystal angel hanging from her window, suspended by a nylon thread. Now the angel was on the floor, broken in two! Astonishingly, however, the nylon thread was still intact, so how on earth could the angel have fallen down?

This event mirrored the one in the hospital room exactly. When Margaret discussed these happenings with Glennyce, they came to the conclusion that they were a sign that Vera no longer had need of these earthly angels as she was now with the real ones!

The funeral for Vera was held at the church where she had worshipped for so many years. Margaret's best friend Maggie, who was close to the family, had been asked to read a lesson during the service. As the funeral procession made its way up the church path and through the doorway, Maggie looked down and saw a lovely, large white feather at her feet. Picking this up, she carried it into the church and held it whilst reading her lesson. Walking back to her seat after reading, Maggie handed the feather to her friend Margaret. It was a tender gesture, and a final message from Vera's angel.

You will not die when your body dies, a part of you goes on.

You will be reunited with your loved ones, because they also are immortal.

Brian L. Weiss M.D.
Psychotherapist and researcher

AFFIRMATION

Today, I align with my angels and see the divinity in each person.

Angel Top Tip

How would you like to be remembered in years to come? With love and happiness, or anxiety and regret? Begin to lay the foundations now for happy memories in the years ahead.

Saying It with Flowers

Whereas some people find it easy to express their feelings for others through tender gestures, others find it difficult to express their love, and we may be left feeling confused and hurt by their apparent coldness towards us. However, we still need to keep an open heart, ready to receive any signs of affection, however unexpected, that may come our way. We may still be surprised by love, as Wendy was:

Having recently lost her mother after a long struggle with cancer, Wendy found herself mulling over their relationship, which had at times been stormy. Looking back, Wendy knew that they had loved each other deeply, even if she had occasionally doubted the fact. Indeed, one of the most difficult aspects of her mother's final days had been that she had not said goodbye to Wendy. In the last few days before her death, Wendy's mother had said goodbye to her sister and told her how much she loved her. Her husband too had been given these assurances, but unfortunately the occasion hadn't arisen in which Wendy's mother had told her how much she loved her. Wendy's upset grew as the days wore on and now her tears flowed constantly.

One day the pain of separation and the fact that her mother's words of love had not been forthcoming seemed to Wendy to be almost too painful to bear. At the height of her distress, the doorbell rang and on opening the door Wendy was handed a beautiful bouquet of flowers. Walking with them back into the house, Wendy noticed their remarkable shape: the flowers were in a teardrop arrangement. Also significant was the fact that the flowers were all pink and white in colour. The bouquet was made from the exact colours and types of flower that Wendy's mother had always bought for her in the past. Pink of course is the colour of love. It was a moving moment and Wendy felt such comfort.

Reading the accompanying card, she realised that the

bouquet had been sent to her by her friend Amelia in America. Amelia was a particularly sensitive lady and clearly had great empathy with her. Wendy rang her friend to say 'thank you' and to explain how helpful the arrival of the flowers had been.

When she heard Amelia's reply, Wendy caught her breath in amazement. Amelia told her that she had wanted to send a more colourful display to cheer her up a little, but was conscious of Wendy's mother 'coming through' and insisting the flowers were those specific colours and shape! Fortunately, Amelia took notice of the message and against her better judgement ordered the flowers. Wendy felt her pain subside. She told her friend about her upset and how thrilled she felt now that, even after death, her mother had found a way of telling her not only that she knew how she felt, but that she loved her very much.

> *Love ever gives,*
>
> *Forgives – outlives,*
>
> *And ever stands with open hands.*

John Oxenham
Journalist, novelist and poet (1852–1941)

Divine Star

Bereavement can be charged with physical, mental and emotional pain. It often feels literally unbearable and we have no idea how we will carry on. But in those dark moments something often happens to soothe or lift our spirits. It may be a kind word from a close friend or a happy memory that suddenly fills our thoughts.

Kallista's Story

If ever there was a story that graphically illustrates the pure nature of love, our final story is the one. Having said that, this story could equally have found a home under the Stars of Courage or Trust. An overwhelming sense of love, however, pervades the entire account. The story also illustrates the fact that love can help ease the heart in the most tragic circumstances. Life, as they say, can turn on a sixpence and the happiest of times can suddenly turn into despair in the blink of an eye. Debby and her family found this to be all too true:

Debby, her husband Tom, and their children Athena, Xander and baby Kallista were looking forward to celebrating Debby's fortieth birthday at Disneyland in Paris as a special treat for all the family. When they arrived in their hotel at the resort, the children were so happy, especially eight-month-old Kallista, who was always smiling. She was a special baby who was loved by all who met her, and her family called her their 'sunshine girl'.

Kallista had never experienced one day's illness in her short life, but sadly the day before Debby's birthday she fell ill. The following morning, when the little girl was no better, her worried parents called the doctor, who decided that she should be admitted to hospital straightaway. Kallista was swiftly taken to the nearest hospital where the doctors decided she was suffering from an asthma attack and treated her accordingly. She showed an encouraging response to the treatment but before the family could sigh with relief her condition suddenly deteriorated. To the shock and horror of her distraught family, and indeed the medical staff, Kallista went into cardiac arrest and died.

Totally numb with shock, Debby and Tom tried to take in what the medical staff were telling them. They were instructed that they had to stay in Paris until an autopsy had been performed. Eventually they established that their little daughter had succumbed to a massive myocarditis infection.

Grief stricken and in a complete daze, these heartbroken parents not only had to come to terms with losing their beloved little daughter, but had to find the strength to keep going for their two other beautiful children. Debby says that amazingly they were given the spiritual guidance and support they needed in this very dark time. This manifested through a series of events.

The first incident occurred when, unable to return home, they had to move from the hotel in Disneyland. Their insurance company found them a hotel that was entirely unsuitable and so they switched to one in a different location. Unfamiliar with Paris, the family had little idea of where they were, but, determined to keep the children's spirits up, they left the hotel for a walk towards the Eiffel Tower. For quite a long time, they could see the top of the tower but didn't appear to be getting any closer to it. Suddenly, precisely when the whole family could view the tower in its entirety, it burst into light. Everyone gasped at the wonderful sight but Debby and Tom privately felt the timing was significant and more than a coincidence.

After an appointment with the coroner, the family felt very low and, taking hold of their children's hands, Tom and Debby found a restaurant for lunch. Walking back to the hotel, little Athena started to chat merrily about all the wonderful things she believed her baby sister Kallista would be enjoying in heaven. Suddenly, Athena came to a halt and stared in disbelief. They all followed her gaze and there in front of them was a shop, painted bright yellow. For them all, the colour yellow represented the sunshine girl and amazingly this shop was called 'Kallista'! It was remarkable, as was the fact that the shop lay only one hundred yards away from their hotel.

Taking stock, Debby explained that they had only been transferred to their hotel at the last minute, and that they had found themselves in a completely unknown part of the city. There was then the fact that 'Kallista' is the most unusual name; they had never seen it written anywhere before, never mind on a shop! This incident lifted their spirits considerably and they took a photograph of their children in front of the shop as a reminder of the amazing coincidence.

This wonderful photograph has proved to be a blessing, but of course returning home was an enormous struggle for the family as they returned to daily life without their dear little baby girl. The entire family was devastated to lose Kallista, and her grandmother, aunt and extended family all keenly felt the loss. However, the signs and the love kept on coming, carrying them through these awful days.

Kallista's grandmother received three wonderful signs from the angels. One night, when she was in real despair, she found a fluffy white feather on her pillow. One morning, when getting dressed for a meeting, she was about to put on her smart suit when she found a lovely little white feather clinging to it, although she had carefully laid it out the night before and checked it was spick and span. The third and final feather was found on a montage of all the grandchildren, resting exactly on the photograph of Kallista. This feather is now safely tucked inside the frame.

One day, Debby's sister said in distress, 'Kallista, you are looking after your mummy and nanny, but what about me?' Continuing with her chores she eventually returned to the spot where she had made her plea, only to find her very own white feather lying there.

The final, very moving sign appeared when Debby was feeling particularly low and decided to take some flowers to Kallista's little plot. The entrance to the cemetery, Debby says, is through a small parkway path. As soon as Debby began to walk along the parkway, she noticed small white feathers on alternate sides of the path. These continued through the cemetery gates, down the cemetery path, only to stop at Kallista's plot! Thrilled and uplifted, Debby told all the family about this magical event. Wanting to see the lovely feathers for themselves, they went along to the cemetery the following day and there the feathers were, still in place. Like all the other feathers that Kallista's family had found, these were small, fluffy and pure white. The whole experience lifted their spirits and Debby says she knows she is not alone during these painful times.

Love is binding the family together; it is reaching down from heaven to earth. Although her family may no longer be able to see Kallista physically, her love and that of the angels will be ever near them.

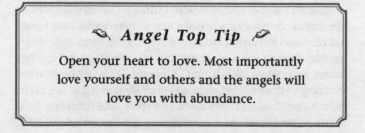

✎ *Angel Top Tip* ✐

Open your heart to love. Most importantly love yourself and others and the angels will love you with abundance.

Life is like a book that never ends, chapters close, but not the book itself.

The end of one physical incarnation is like the end of a chapter, on some level setting up the beginning of another.

Marianne Williamson
Spiritual activist, author and lecturer

With Love We Can Make It

As the Beatles sang, 'All you need is love' . . . Love is the very core of life and without it our lives have little meaning. From the very moment of our birth, love guides us, nurtures us and helps us to grow. It ensures our meaningful interaction with others. It fascinates and engages our understanding and compassion. Enriching our relationships with parents, children, friends, the natural world and even our pets, love is all-encompassing. It guides us through life and eases our death.

As long as we continue to love, we can never be separated from anyone. In the immortal words of St Paul, writing to the Corinthians: ' . . . though I speak with the tongues of men and angels and have not love, I am as a sounding brass or tinkling symbol. And though I have the gift of prophecy and understand all mysteries and all knowledge and though I have all faith so that I could remove mountains and have not love, I am nothing.' If you are going to wish upon a star, make that star the Star of Love.

STAR POINTS TO PONDER:

I love myself.

I love life.

I am worthy of love.

I show love to others.

I give and receive love.

I reach out to others in need.

I know that love is eternal.

Conclusion

An Eternity of Stars

*I*f we are determined, our journeys through life can be exciting and rewarding in spite of whatever obstacles may be put in our paths. As the stories in this book show, many people are tried and tested in the extreme and yet these same individuals often find comfort and courage in adversity through the simplest of means. They trust the angelic signs and messages that appear to them, and against all the odds they find themselves counting their blessings.

We sincerely hope that these seven chapters have inspired, soothed and encouraged you to count your own blessings. Take comfort in the fact that the angels are there for you as they are for everybody. Should you begin to work seriously on improving your self-belief, with true courage, the angels will work with you to ensure your success. Grasp the nettle, determine that from this day on you will be positive, trusting and courageous. This attitude will in turn encourage harmony and peace in your daily life, and with that sense of fulfilment comes love.

Know that you are here for a reason: to bring forth self-belief, harmony, gratitude, trust, courage, peace and love into the world. Embrace this journey of belief and healing. Look to the stars and to your angels, but also look inside yourself. There you shall find your inner angels and all the answers you will ever need. Most importantly . . .

believe and receive

STAR POINTS TO PONDER:

I am aware of my stars and angels.

I believe in myself.

I harmonise my life.

I am grateful for my blessings.

I trust in a Higher Power.

I am courageous; this is my life.

I am a child of the Universe.

Further Reading

Carter-Scott, Cherie, *If Life is a Game, These are the Rules* (Broadway Books, 1998)

Chopra, Deepak, *The Seven Spiritual Laws of Success* (Bantam Press, 1996)

Chopra, Deepak, *The Deeper Wound* (Rider Books, 2001)

Covey, Stephen, *The 7 Habits of Highly Effective People* (Simon & Schuster Ltd, 1999)

Davis, Annie, *The Little Book of Miracles* (McDougal Publishing, 1998)

His Holiness Dalai Lama and Culter C. Howard, MD, *The Art of Happiness* (Riverhead Books, 1998)

Drucker, Peter, *The Essential Drucker* (HarperCollins, 2003)

Dyer, Wayne W., *Real Magic* (HarperCollins, 1994)

Foundation for Inner Peace, *A Course in Miracles* (Arkana, 1997)

Gawain, Shakti, *Creative Visualization* (Whatever Publishing, 1997)

Gibran, Kahlil, *The Prophet* (Arrow, 1998)

Graves, Robert, *The White Goddess* (Metropolitan Books, 1997)

Hay, Louise, *You Can Heal Your Life* (Hay House Inc, 2002)

— *Everyday Positive Thinking* (Hay House Inc, 2004)

Holmes, Ernest, *How to Use the Science of Mind* (Dodd, Mead and Co, 1950)

Jeffers, Susan, *Feel the Fear and Do It Anyway* (Vermilion, 2007)

Lensink, Marianne, *Guided Coincidences* (Schors Publishing, 2006)

McClure, Vimala, *Tao of Motherhood* (New World Library, 1992)

Nacson, Leon, *A Stream of Dreams* (Hay House Inc, 2003)

Ponder, Catherine, *Prosperity Power of Prayer* (De Vorss & Company, 1984)

Richardson, Cheryl, *Take Time for Your Life* (Broadway Books, 2000)

Rinpoche, Sogyal, *The Tibetan Book of Living and Dying* (Rider Books, 2002)

Ruiz, Don Miguel, *The Four Agreements* (Amber-Allen Publishing, 1997)

Smiley, Tavis, *Empowerment Cards for Inspired Living* (Hay House Inc, 2004)

Weiss, Brian L., *Many Lives, Many Masters* (Piatkus Books, 1994)

Williamson, Marianne, *A Return to Love* (HarperCollins, 1996)

Wilson Schaef, Anne, *Meditations for Women Who Do Too Much* (HarperOne, 2004)

Useful Addresses

For more information about Glennyce Eckersley, visit:
www.glennyceeckersley.com

For more information about Gary Quinn, visit:
www.garyquinn.tv

For information regarding books about life after death, visit:
www.amazon.co.uk

For information about the work of the Cancer Aid &
Listening Line, visit: www.canceraid.co.uk

For information about Suzannah James's music (see Star of
Harmony, page 72), visit: www.purleychasecentre.org.uk

For workshops based on the number seven, contact Rev.
David Gaffney at david.gaffney@general conference.org.uk

Acknowledgements

Whenever a book reaches completion, it gives rise to such a feeling of gratitude that to say simply thank you feels inadequate. I hope the special people involved in the production of this book realise just how special they are, and how very grateful we feel for their continuing support, encouragement and guidance. Thank you to:

Judith Kendra, Sue Lascelles, Sarah Bennie, Caroline Newbury, Ed Griffiths, David Parrish, Ross Eckersley, Rachel Eckersley, Ed Potten, Gillian Smith, Michael Smith, Rev. Gillian Gordon, Jean Thornton, Val Bagarozzi, August Bagarozzi, Mary Bullough, Greta Woolf, Stella Morris and all the staff at Sweetens Book Store, Janice Green, Barbara Moulton, Evelyn M. Dalton, Fern Britton, Philip Schofield, Rev. David Gaffney, Leeza Gibbons, Anne Taylor, Cheryl Murphy, Christopher Watt, Vivien Gibson, Bryan Craig, Cheryl Welch, Patty Q., Circa De La Cruz, Fiona Harrold, Kelly Wald, Jane Gibson of Brightlight, Pam Beldon, Jason Kinrade, Wendy Price, Beverly Aldritt, Doriana Mazola, Sante Losio, Kenny Feuerman, Sherry Daech, Patty Fleming, Christine Miller R.Q., Sarah, Cindy Schneider, Michiko J. Rolek, Amelia Kinkade, Harold Dupre, Bruce Hatton, Patricia McDonough, Brian Wright and Shannon Factor, Trish and Steve Watt, Kim and Johan Uyttewaal, Ute Ville, Ikuko Iwasaki, Douglas Preston, Elizabeth Day and Anna Ouroumian.

Lastly and by no means least, a huge thank you to the kind and generous people who allow us to include their special and personal stories; they are:

Patsy Allen, Christina Aspinall, Anne Bailey, Lynn Barrat, Frank Berwick, Kath Braden, Marie Caltieri, Norma Clarke, Pamela Cuthbert, Roy Cuthbert, Jane Dale, Steven Evans,

Barbara Evans, Julie Fearnhead, Debby, Tom, Athena, and
Xander Heavey, Margaret Hindley, Rebecca Holt, Kelly
Horton, Suzannah James, Marianne Lensink, Bernard Mason,
Louise Metcalf, Norma Mosley, Nancy Moss, Janice O'Gara,
Trisha Peacock, Dulcie Pembeiro, Margaret Porter, Wendy
Price, Gemma Procter, Stephanie Rose, Colin Sheldon, Sarah
Sheldon, Carter Stewart-Singleton, Marjorie Taylor, Enid
Wardleworth, Louise Wilson, also William, Helen and
Hannah.

Also available from Rider Books

Angel Awakenings

Bring the Angels into Your Life Each Day of the Year

Glennyce S. Eckersley & Gary Quinn

Wake up to the angels! You can give an angelic sparkle to your whole day by dipping into this special book each morning.

In this heavenly almanac, leading angel expert Glennyce S. Eckersley recalls amazing true stories about angels, revealing how they help and protect us. And world-renowned intuitive life coach Gary Quinn suggests many practical ways to attract a glittering celestial presence into your life.

You too can experience how the angels are by your side every day, each month of the year, guiding you through the changing seasons and watching over you with love.

Buy Rider Books

Order further Rider titles from your local bookshop or have them delivered direct to your door by Bookpost.

❑ *Angel Awakenings* 9781846040610 £8.99
  by Glennyce S. Eckersley & Gary Quinn

❑ *An Angel Forever* 9781844135790 £7.99
  by Glennyce S. Eckersley & Gary Quinn

❑ *An Angel at My Shoulder* 9781846040658 £6.99
  by Glennyce S. Eckersley

❑ *May the Angels Be with You* 9780712610728 £6.99
  by Gary Quinn

Free Post and Packing
Overseas customers allow £2.00 per paperback

Order
By phone: 01624 677237
By post: Random House Books c/o Bookpost, PO Box 29, Douglas, Isle of Man, IM99 1BQ
By fax: 01624 670923
By email: bookshop@enterprise.net
Cheques (payable to Bookpost) and credit cards accepted

Prices and availability subject to change without notice. Allow 28 days for delivery. When placing your order, please mention if you do not wish to receive any additional information.

www.rbooks.co.uk